Wishing / 'the best.
Love,
Bob

My Life with Faulkner and Brodsky

Robert W. Hamblin

Published for the Center for Faulkner Studies by
Southeast Missouri State University Press | 2017

My Life with Faulkner and Brodsky
by Robert W. Hamblin

Copyright 2017 by Robert W. Hamblin

Softcover: $15.00
ISBN: 978-0-9979262-2-4

First published in 2017 by
Southeast Missouri State University Press
One University Plaza, MS 2650
Cape Girardeau, MO 63701
www.semopress.com

Cover Design: Carrie M. Walker

Photographs by Paul Lueders. Courtesy of Special Collections.
Southeast Missouri State University

Contents

School Days

You may be surprised to learn that we didn't read William Faulkner in the high school classrooms of Baldwyn and Booneville, Mississippi, in the 1950s. Surely at least one of our English teachers must have known that a writer living only seventy miles to the west of us had been awarded the Nobel Prize for Literature in December 1950, but that information never penetrated the walls of our classrooms. Later I would learn that many of his neighbors in Oxford—and even some of his relatives—had an extremely low opinion of "Count No 'Count," as Faulkner was sometimes called; but at least his fellow townsmen acknowledged his existence and knew that he was a writer. In Baldwyn and Booneville it was as if he had never been born.

Nevertheless, though I had no way of knowing it at the time, I was being prepared in my childhood and youth for my lifelong reading of Faulkner. The front porch of my parents' general store at Brice's Cross Roads was much like the porch of Varner's store in Frenchman's Bend, the setting of Faulkner's 1940 novel, *The Hamlet*. There, local farmers gathered when the fields were too wet to plow or the cotton had been laid by or crops had been harvested. There, they swapped stories, played checkers and dominos, and spat tobacco juice onto the graveled road that came right up to the front steps. My maternal grandfather, Pappy Hickey, often sat on the storefront at Brice's Cross Roads and, like the old-timers in Faulkner's family and fiction, told stories of the Civil War as they had been handed down from generation to generation.

"Granddad was a wagon driver for General Forrest and served with him the whole war," Pappy Hickey told a *Chicago Tribune* reporter who interviewed him in 1950. "On the day before the battle he drove his wagon, loaded with corn for Forrest's horses, up to the farm on Tishomingo Creek and called the family out into the yard. 'You'll have to get away from here,' he told my grandmother, 'because there's going to be a battle here tomorrow.' But my dad wasn't the type to run from a fight, so he clumb a tree and cheered and hollered while Forrest whupped them Yankees like they never been whupped afore. After the battle Dad came here to Bethany Church just over there behind the Brice house, and counted 17 Yankees who had crawled under the floor of the church to die."

So, years later, when I read Uncle Buck McCaslin's boastful remarks about the legendary Confederate colonel John Sartoris in *The Unvanquished*—"Heard of him? . . . Who ain't heard of him in this country? Get the Yankees to tell you about him sometime"—it was my grandfather's voice I heard in my head.

My contacts with African American neighbors and playmates also provided a helpful context for my later reading of Faulkner's novels and stories. My close friendship with one black playmate, Sonny Agnew, was not unlike the relationship between Bayard Sartoris and Ringo in *The Unvanquished*, although the only contacts Sonny and I had with war of any kind were the battlefield games we played in and around the park that memorialized the Union and Confederate soldiers who fought in the Battle of Brice's Cross Roads, as well as our visits to the graves of the Confederate soldiers buried in the Presbyterian cemetery just down the road. Sonny was the only one of us boys brave enough to ride our homemade cart down a steep hill, the trip ending with the cart smashed to pieces and Sonny rolling on the ground, laughing. Araminta, the African American woman who helped my mother wash clothes in the huge black pot in the back yard and also helped her at hog-killing time cook out the lard and cracklings and grind the sausage, was the first Dilsey, the black servant of *The Sound and the Fury*, I ever knew. Unlike the Compsons, my mother never asked anyone to come to our back door, and Araminta often sat with Mama and me at our kitchen table, eating lunch with us.

I would even include in my preparation for reading Faulkner my boyhood love affair with the Brooklyn Dodgers. Probably the only white Dodgers fan in all of Mississippi, I cheered for Jackie and Campy and Newk and, as a result, was sometimes called a "nigger lover" by some of my playmates—just as Faulkner was by some of his fellow citizens.

I knew only one other individual who was also a Dodgers fan— John, the black handyman who worked for Prather Auto Company, the Ford and Standard Oil dealer in Baldwyn, where my father also worked, driving a gas and oil delivery truck. During the summer months, I sometimes accompanied Daddy on his deliveries, and between runs I would often visit with the salesmen, mechanics, and other workers in the office or garage. John, the only black employee, washed and waxed cars, pumped gas and fixed flats, cleaned the floors, and emptied the trash. Called "Nigger John" by most whites, sometimes even in his presence, to me he was a prince of a man—a soft-spoken, polite, and gentle soul elevated to royalty in my eyes because he shared my love for the Dodgers. "Jackie got two hits yesterday," he would say, or "Campy hit a home run," and we would replay the games while I helped him chamois a car he had just washed. Looking back, I see us as comrades in arms, a white child and a middle-aged, deferential black man, underdogs and confederates conducting guerrilla warfare against a prejudiced and unjust majority. I don't recall ever being told his last name, but I shall never forget how his face brightened and his voice became more animated when we talked of Jackie, Campy, and Newk.

Then there is the parallel of language in Faulkner's books. Even today, when I read Faulkner's renditions of Southern dialect, white or black, I hear again the voices from the front porches and schoolrooms and cotton fields and churches of my childhood.

But, of course, I didn't know any of that at the time. I fell in love with reading at an early age, but my standard fare was western novels, particularly the Lone Ranger and Red Ryder series, or sports stories, like the Chip Hilton books. My sixth-grade teacher, Mrs. Bloodworth, advanced my literary appreciation a bit by requiring her class to memorize and recite a poem each week, a few of which—such as "In Flanders Field," "My Shadow," and "Wynken, Blynken, and Nod"—I can still partially quote six decades later. The first classic novel I ever read—on the recommendation of a seventh-grade classmate, not a teacher—was an abridged version of Victor Hugo's *Les Miserables*. After that I was eternally hooked on words and stories and in high school found myself eagerly feasting on Shakespeare's poetry and dramaturgy: *Julius Caesar* in Mrs. Martha Ruth Martin's tenth-grade English class and *Macbeth* in Mrs. Marian Young's eleventh-grade English class.

But still, no Faulkner. That didn't change when I enrolled at Northeast Mississippi Junior College in my hometown of Booneville, where we had moved when we left the Cross Roads. At Northeast, I studied English literature with a brilliant and inspirational teacher, J.C. Pardue, but since that was British literature, there was no place for Faulkner in the syllabus. Though a Mississippian, Mr. Pardue read Keats and Wordsworth in a precise, clipped, perfect English accent (or so it seemed to me) that made the poems sing and me wish that I were in England (as one day I would be). Nevertheless, though Mr. Pardue was one of my finest teachers and greatly contributed to my love and appreciation of literature, I never once heard him mention William Faulkner.

After being graduated from the junior college, I transferred to Delta State College in Cleveland, in the heart of the Mississippi Delta; and there it was, in my junior year in the spring of 1959, that I first heard of Faulkner.

That semester I enrolled in a class in Southern Literature, taught by Dr. Thomas Daniel Young, an outstanding scholar who would later become the Gertrude C. Vanderbilt Professor of English at Vanderbilt University. Dr. Young was the co-editor—with Richmond Croom Beatty, Floyd C. Watkins, and Randall Stewart—of the textbook we used, *The Literature of the South*. That book, which still holds its honored place on my bookshelf, includes three selections from Faulkner: the short stories "That Evening Sun Go Down" and "An Odor of Verbena" and the Nobel Prize Acceptance Speech. My penciled underlinings and marginal notations in the book evidence that I read all three selections quite closely, and these readings were my first introduction to the writings of William Faulkner.

I don't recall any of Dr. Young's remarks about these stories or Faulkner's magnificent speech, but I do recall a personal story he told about his own discovery of Faulkner. A native of Louisville, Mississippi, Dr. Young served as an Army intelligence officer in France during World War II. There he met quite a few academics and intellectuals, and when they found out he was from Mississippi, they wanted to talk with him about that Mississippi writer Faulkner. Sadly, and to the amazement of his French compatriots, he had to confess that he knew nothing of Faulkner. But, Dr. Young told our class, when the war was over and he returned stateside, one of the first places he went was to a library to check out some books by Faulkner. He quickly learned why the French were so excited about his fellow Mississippian, and now he was passing on his enthusiasm for this author to his students.

I was so impressed by the Faulkner selections we read in that Southern Literature class, and by Dr. Young's endorsement of Faulkner, that I chose to write my term paper that semester on Faulkner's *As I Lay Dying*. While I had been moved by Nancy's plight in "That Evening Sun Go Down," impressed by Bayard Sartoris's courage and sense of honor in "An Odor of Verbena," and of course uplifted by the poetic phrasing of the Nobel Prize Speech, none of that prepared me for the immense pleasure and awe I experienced as I turned the pages of *As I Lay Dying*. I had never read, or couldn't even have imagined, a story told in this fashion. As readers of the novel well know, Faulkner tosses the narration of this novel around like a football on a playground. First Darl speaks, and then Cora, and then Darl again, and then Jewel. Eventually we learn, if we bother to keep count, that there are fifteen different narrators and fifty-nine separate chapters in the novel. Fortunately, the story line presented is a fairly simple one: a rural Mississippi family, the Bundrens, are taking the corpse of Addie, the wife and mother, back to her hometown of Jefferson to be buried with her family. So it's not the plot but the way Faulkner chooses to unravel the plot that makes this such a complicated and intriguing novel.

And why would anyone choose to tell a story in this manner? The principal result of Faulkner's shifting the storytelling from one character to another is fairly easy to identify—and quite compelling. We know from our own experience that if two or more people observe the same event, they will see it—and later recount it—somewhat or perhaps even quite differently. Anyone who has served on a jury knows how a parade of witnesses, some friendly, some hostile, offer varying and often contradictory versions of the same event. And the juror must decide what actually happened and who's telling the truth and who isn't. It's the same with this novel, with the reader playing the role of the juror. Is Cora right about which of the sons is Addie's favorite? What is Anse's real reason for wanting to go to Jefferson? Why is Jewel so angry and spiteful? What is Darl's problem? Answers to such questions depend on who's talking—and who's reading. Clearly what Faulkner is conveying here is not an absolute, "capital-T" Truth but a "little-t" truth that depends in large measure on narrative viewpoint.

I had never before been so taken with the way an author chooses to tell a story; and with that reading of *As I Lay Dying*, I began what became a career-long interest in Faulkner's technique—not so much the stories Faulkner tells as the way he chooses to tell them. Henry James once remarked that there must be a thousand different ways to tell a story, and, as I continued reading Faulkner in the years to come, I became convinced that he was determined to experiment with every single one of those methods.

At Ole Miss

Following my graduation from Delta State College in 1960, I married my high school and college sweetheart, Kaye Smith; and shortly after, the two of us headed for Baltimore, Maryland, where we both had contracted for teaching positions—hers as a first-grade teacher and mine as an eleventh-grade English teacher and assistant baseball coach. We knew these would be temporary employments, affording us the time to settle into our marriage, see a different part of the country, and begin to make our plans for graduate school, to which both of us were committed. After teaching two years in the Baltimore County Public Schools, we considered several options for graduate study but finally decided to return to Mississippi, where I would enroll in the doctoral program in American literature at the University of Mississippi and she would teach first grade in nearby Batesville, earn her "Ph.T." ("Putting Hubby Through"), and work on her master's degree in education on the side.

I owe my enrollment at Ole Miss partly to the Russian satellite Sputnik. When the Russians sent the first manufactured satellite into orbit in 1957, they initiated the "Space Race," which ultimately saw Americans land a man on the moon. The U.S.'s response to the Russians' success with Sputnik was to create and encourage programs in science and technology that would produce more Ph.D.'s and thus enable the U.S. to compete with the Russians in the exploration of outer space. A major result of this emphasis was the passage of the National Defense Education Act in 1958, Title IV of which was designed to alleviate an existing shortage of qualified college teachers. Most of the funds made available by this provision went to the training of math and science teachers, but (politics being politics) some of the money was allowed to trickle down to programs in the humanities. The University of Mississippi utilized available NDEA funding to develop doctoral programs in a number of areas, including English; and I was fortunate to be among the school's early recipients of an NDEA fellowship.

Throughout the spring of 1962, as I finished out my second year of teaching and coaching at Sparrows Point High School, I eagerly anticipated our move to Oxford, greatly excited by the prospect of living in the hometown of William Faulkner, by then one of my favorite authors. Surely I would get to see him on the streets of Oxford and perhaps even chance to meet and talk with him. Such was not to be, however, as Faulkner died on July 6, a little more than a month before our planned arrival in Oxford. I heard the news on the radio in Baltimore, as Kaye and I were already beginning to pack our things and ready for our return to our native state. The sadness I felt over the death of one of the world's most gifted writers was heightened by my personal disappointment that now I would never get to see or meet the great man. That disappointment became keener a few months later when I learned that Professor James Webb, chairman of the English department at Ole Miss, had arranged for Faulkner to visit some literature classes at Ole Miss during the upcoming school year. Some things, as they say, just aren't meant to be.

As events unfolded, though, the presence of Faulkner turned out to be more real to me during my days at Ole Miss than I could ever have desired, or even anticipated—more real in some ways than if I had been privileged to meet the man himself. As coincidence would have it, my first semester of graduate study coincided with the riot that accompanied the enrollment of James Meredith, the first African American student to attend Ole Miss. And, more coincidence, three years later, my last semester at Ole Miss was marked by another racial incident, the near-riot that occurred when some African American students from Tougaloo College attended the Southern Literary Festival hosted that year by Ole Miss.

I had close-up views of both of these events. During the Meredith crisis, I was one of the hundreds of Mississippi National Guardsmen federalized by President Kennedy and sent to the campus to help in restoring order. During the 1965 Southern Literary Festival, I was asked by the English Department to serve as the personal escort for Robert Penn Warren, one of the principal speakers at the Festival, and thus I had the opportunity to observe firsthand Warren's response to the mistreatment of the Tougaloo students. In between these events, there were other mini-crises on campus, as Ole Miss adapted to the new world of integration and expanded civil rights for African Americans.

For me personally, all of these events were viewed and interpreted through the lens of my study of Faulkner under the expert guidance of

Dr. John Pilkington. I signed up for Dr. Pilkington's Faulkner seminar, and my experiences in that class led to my writing a master's thesis and eventually a doctoral dissertation on Faulkner's works, both directed by Dr. Pilkington. Given the explosive racial environment of my three years at Ole Miss, my reading of Faulkner's writings on race took on sharper meaning and intensity. The lynching of Joe Christmas, the saintliness of Dilsey Gibson, the Negrophobia of Thomas Sutpen, the growing racial awareness of Ike McCaslin, the stubborn pride and insistence of Lucas Beauchamp, the youthful courage of Chick Mallison—all such fictional behaviors and characters, it seemed, had sprung to life in actuality. Never before or since have my reading and formal education been so highly charged with existential experience, giving everything I read or studied an enhanced relevance and significance.

As an aside, I should note that Faulkner was not the only great Mississippi author that Dr. Pilkington had his students read. We also read Richard Wright, and his novel *Native Son* provided another corrective lens through which I viewed the day-to-day events now unfolding at Ole Miss.

In reading *Native Son* I was reminded that I had never met, in my Mississippi childhood and adolescence, a Bigger Thomas or a Richard Wright—that is, an openly militant black man who was fed up with the old system and refused to accept it any longer. But now just such a black man had pushed his way into the same space that I occupied, demanding his equal share of that space. James Meredith was not the violent, vengeful rebel that Bigger Thomas is, but he shared the same anger and frustration at the African American's plight, and he was just as determined, though fortunately in a more positive and productive manner, to register his protest against the status quo. It seemed clear to me that, in his quiet courage and grim determination to claim his constitutional rights, Meredith was a later incarnation of that same black spirit and pride that Richard Wright had written about two decades earlier and which led him to coin the phrase "Black Power."

And so it continued for an entire year. It seemed that my participation in the enforced integration of Ole Miss and the physical proximity of James Meredith throughout the 1962–63 school year affected almost everything I did, said, or thought. It was as though somehow the principle and condition of being Negro had wedged its way into my life and consciousness, indeed into my very soul, in a way that it never had before—despite my growing up in the South—altering forever my views of race, democracy, justice, and the world.

Along with my reading of the New Testament and African American literature, especially the works of Richard Wright and James Baldwin, my study of Faulkner's novels and stories helped me—a white Southerner raised in segregation—navigate the troubled waters that, with integration and the Civil Rights Movement, swept across Ole Miss, Mississippi, the South, and the entire nation. Faulkner—and his characters such as Ike McCaslin and Chick Mallison—helped me and many others come to realize that these waters represented not a drowning but a baptism, a death and burial of old, outdated, unjust ways, and a resurrection to a new and better life.

I'm still disappointed that I never got to see or meet William Faulkner, but I'm very grateful that his words and books were there to enlighten and inspire me during that difficult time, and they have remained with me every day of my adult life and career.

My three years of graduate study at Ole Miss enabled me not only to study Faulkner's writings in depth under the mentorship of an outstanding, Harvard-educated literary scholar but also to immerse myself in Faulkner's locale, as well as to get to know several of his friends and relatives. I could walk the Oxford Square and sit on the benches on the courthouse lawn, where Faulkner also walked and sat with his fellow townsmen. On the south side of the courthouse, I could view the statue of the Confederate soldier and find amusement, just as Faulkner does in *Requiem for a Nun*, that the soldier seems to be in retreat, his back turned to his Northern foes. On the east side of the Square sat the stately red-brick post office, where Faulkner daily checked his mail; on the north side, the building that had been his grandfather's bank, where a young Faulkner worked briefly as an accountant, in the process learning, as he later phrased it, "the medicinal value of his [grandfather's] liquor." On the northwest corner was Sneed's Hardware, the balcony of which housed the room that served as Gavin Stevens's law office in the film version of *Intruder in the Dust*; on the south side, Gathright-Reed's Drug Store, where Faulkner regularly stopped by to chat with his good friend Mac Reed and sometimes leaf through the paperback copies of murder mysteries displayed on the store's book rack. Looming over all of these, magnificent and grand, its white cupola shining brilliantly against a blue summer sky, was the Lafayette County Courthouse, the hub of Faulkner's Yoknapatawpa.

Just off the square to the west was the small Victorian cottage that housed the law office of Phil Stone, Faulkner's good friend and mentor, whose secretary typed many of Faulkner's early poems and stories. A few blocks south of the square was the Chandler house and grounds, where Faulkner observed through the wrought-iron fence a mentally challenged adult who became the prototype for one of the most famous characters in American literature, Benjy Compson. Northeast of the square was St. Peter's Cemetery, which includes the Falkner family plot and, just down the hill in the newer section of the cemetery, the grave that holds the remains of Faulkner. There Faulkner lies at the foot of an ancient oak tree, and standing there, one recalls the last lines of the epitaph a young Faulkner wrote for himself when he thought he wouldn't live past thirty years of age: "Where is there the death / While in these blue hills slumberous overhead / I'm rooted like a tree? Though I be dead, / This soil that holds me fast will find me breath."

From the edge of the Ole Miss campus, I could take the mile-long path through Bailey's Woods to Rowan Oak, Faulkner's home on the southern outskirts of the town. After Faulkner's death, his widow, Estelle, moved from Oxford to live with one of her children, and she left it to her sister, Dorothy Oldham, to look after Rowan Oak. Andrew Price, an elderly black handyman who lived with his family in the cabin behind the big house, maintained the house and grounds. Though Rowan Oak would not be opened for public viewing until several years later, in those days one could ignore the No Trespassing sign, stroll the grounds, and lean on the paddock fence to talk with Andrew about his recollections of "Mister Bill." Today Rowan Oak and its grounds are crowded with tourists and other visitors, but when I was at Ole Miss, before the University acquired the property and opened it as a national historic site, the place elicited a solitude and serenity that seemed to invite intimate communication with Faulkner's spirit.

Faulkner purchased the Old Shegog Place in 1930, shortly after he married Estelle Oldham Franklin. At the time, the old house, built in 1849, was dilapidated and rundown, with farm animals occupying a part of the building. Faulkner christened the place Rowan Oak, after the legendary tree that is thought to bring good luck, and began the process of restoring the house to something of its antebellum glory. A couple of years later he purchased the adjacent twenty-nine acres of heavily wooded land known as Bailey's Woods. In my time in Oxford, these woods were interlaced with horseback riding trails that Faulkner had created for himself and his daughter Jill to use.

Faulkner's sister-in-law, Dorothy Oldham, was the curator of the Mississippi Room in the Ole Miss library. It was in that room that I conducted much of my research for both my master's thesis and my doctoral dissertation, so I came to know "Miss Dot" quite well. It was rumored that if she did not approve of your Faulkner topic, she wouldn't assist you in your research. Apparently she approved of my topics, since she cooperated fully with me, not only in locating and providing research materials but also in sharing Faulkner family stories.

Still, I was a lowly graduate student, and Miss Dot was a member of the Oxford aristocracy (at least in her own mind), so I had to be careful to mind my manners and remember my place. I learned that lesson early in my dealings with Miss Dot, but it was driven home indisputably in the spring of 1965, when, as noted previously, I served as Robert Penn Warren's personal guide during the meeting of the Southern Literary Festival. At that time Rowan Oak was still a private residence, though unoccupied, but I arranged for Miss Dot to open and show the home to Warren. At the appointed hour, I drove Warren to Rowan Oak and escorted him to the front door, where we were met by Miss Dot. Smiling, dressed in a formal evening gown even though it was the middle of the afternoon, she welcomed Warren into the house—and then promptly closed the door in my face. I had previously escorted Warren to a cocktail hour and a dinner party, and had been made to feel welcome at each of those, so I presumed I would accompany him as well on his tour of Rowan Oak. But Miss Dot had other ideas, so for the next hour I was left to sit on the front steps and walk the grounds while Miss Dot hosted Warren inside the house.

As I drove Warren back to the Alumni House where he was staying, he expressed consternation and regret over my rude treatment by Miss Dot. I just laughed and told him, "That's Miss Dot. We're all used to her behavior by now."

Malcolm Cowley, the editor of *The Portable Faulkner*, the publication of which, some say, rescued Faulkner's literary career from obscurity, was also a presenter at the 1965 Southern Literary Festival. One afternoon when Mr. Warren did not require my services, I asked Cowley if he would like to meet Faulkner's good friend, Mac Reed. Yes, certainly, Cowley replied, so I drove him to the town square and escorted him to Mr. Reed's office in the back of the Gathright-Reed Drug Store. Then, for the next hour (Mr. Reed being more polite than Ms. Oldham), I sat and listened as one of America's most influential literary critics and one of Faulkner's closest personal friends discussed the world-renowned writer—and I didn't take a single note on the conversation!

Murry "Chooky" Falkner (who never added the *u* to his name), nephew of the famous novelist, operated an insurance agency in Oxford and was also the company commander of the local Mississippi National Guard unit. That unit was the first to arrive on campus to defend the federal marshals and James Meredith on the night of the infamous riot. When the Baldwyn unit, of which I was a member, arrived on campus later that same evening, the battle between the marshals and the mob was already fully joined. As we unloaded from our troop carriers immediately in front of the Lyceum Building, we saw that a bulldozer, now abandoned, had been driven toward the front of the building. Years later, in reading Dean Faulkner Wells's *Time by the Sun*, I learned the identity of the driver of the bulldozer—Jimmy Faulkner. Thus the two brothers, Jimmy and Chooky, nephews of Faulkner, found themselves on opposite sides of the integration crisis, just as their father and uncle also were.

During my time in Oxford, I became good friends with Chooky Falkner, initially because of our shared membership in the Mississippi National Guard and subsequently because of my interest in the literary works of William Faulkner. Regarding the latter, Chooky never missed an opportunity to chide me for my obsession with his uncle; his father, John Fa(u)lkner, was by far the better writer, Chooky insisted. I place the "u" in parenthesis because, unlike other members of the family, John could never quite settle on which spelling of the name to use. In fact, on his gravestone in St. Peter's Cemetery, one side of the monument shows "Faulkner," the other side shows "Falkner," and the ground marker shows "Fa(u)lkner"!

In later years both Chooky and his brother Jimmy (who did add the *u* to his name) became regular presenters at the annual Faulkner and Yoknapatawpha Conference, recounting stories of Faulkner's days in Oxford. And still later, after the creation of our Center for Faulkner Studies at Southeast Missouri State University, I hosted Chooky's visit to our campus to talk about his famous uncle. As a part of that program, Chooky allowed our Center to print and sell a limited issue print of the painting his father had drawn of a scene in Faulkner's short story "Red Leaves."

During the later years of our friendship, Chooky liked to point out that he was the first Falkner to attain the rank of general in the armed forces, having been promoted to that rank in the Mississippi National Guard. The old colonel, Chooky reminded me, had sought the rank of general in the Confederate army but failed to secure it; his uncle had failed to earn his wings as a member of the RAF; and his brother

Jimmy had been a lieutenant in World War II and afterward became a colonel in the Naval Reserve. But now, in Chooky, the Falkner family had their general.

In Oxford I met many others who knew Faulkner, either personally or just from a distance as a fellow townsman. These included James Silver, the Ole Miss history professor who, along with his wife, Dutch, was a close friend of the Faulkners; Aston Holley, who as a boy had been a member of the Boy Scouts troop for which Faulkner served as scoutmaster; A. Wigfall Green, my Chaucer and Middle English professor, who had published one of the first scholarly articles on Faulkner (in the *Sewanee Review* in 1932 and which, by the way, perpetuated the erroneous stories of Faulkner's participation in World War I); and James W. Webb, the chairman of the Ole Miss English department, who would become the first curator of Rowan Oak. According to Joseph Blotner, it was Dr. Webb who found the "Rowan Oak papers," a group of Faulkner manuscripts, in a closet in Faulkner's home—although, in actuality, it was a graduate school classmate of mine, Beverly Smith, Dr. Webb's assistant curator, who discovered the manuscripts—while emptying a closet in preparation for the Orkin man to spray for insects!

I left Ole Miss in the late summer of 1965 and accepted a teaching position at Southeast Missouri State University. As an "A.B.D."—"All But the Dissertation"—I anticipated that I would complete my dissertation, devote myself to my teaching duties, and, except for occasionally teaching one of his stories or novels to my students, put Faulkner behind me. How could I know that such was not to be.

ENTER BRODSKY

In the fall semester of 1977, I taught a graduate seminar in the American novel, including Faulkner's *The Sound and the Fury*. One student in the class was Bob Benham, an English teacher at Farmington High School, a little more than an hour's drive northwest of Cape Girardeau. During a break in our discussion of Faulkner's novel, Bob asked me if I had ever met L.D. Brodsky, the Faulkner collector who lived in Farmington. I said no; in fact, I was quite surprised to learn that there was a Faulkner collector in Missouri. Curious, I asked Bob if he could provide me with contact information for Brodsky. At the next class session Bob brought me Mr. Brodsky's mailing address.

I immediately wrote a letter to Brodsky, introducing myself and describing my longtime study of Faulkner's works. Then I waited—and waited, and waited. Some three months later, after I had very nearly forgotten about making the inquiry, I heard back. L.D. apologized for taking so long to answer my letter, explaining that he had been tied up with business affairs, that he and his wife, Jan, were busy adjusting to the arrival of their second child, and that his family was just returning from an extended vacation in Florida, where, I later learned, the Brodsky family owned a condominium. He then invited me to visit him in Farmington at the nearest opportunity, so we could meet one another and discuss our mutual interest in Faulkner.

On a Saturday morning in March 1978, I drove to Farmington to meet with Brodsky. He had instructed me to meet him in the lobby of the Mercantile Bank on the town square. I arrived a little early and took a seat that offered a good view of the front door. I wondered what this Faulkner collector would look like, how old he was, whether I could guess his identity when he entered the bank. I didn't have to wait long, and I knew it was he as soon as he stepped inside the door. He was of medium height, muscularly built, with alert, friendly eyes and long, curly, Afro-styled brown hair. He was casually dressed, wearing slacks and a polo shirt open at the neck, revealing a large gold necklace. His most distinguishable characteristic was a long handlebar moustache, immaculately waxed and curled on each end. He paused just inside the door, scanned the room to find the only stranger there, and walked toward me. Neither of us could know that that first handshake would be the beginning of a thirty-six year collaboration and friendship. Looking back, I now know it was one of the luckiest days of my life.

After a brief exchange of greetings, L.D. led me down a hallway to a conference room where we took seats at a long table. L.D. asked me about my interest in Faulkner; I told him about my graduate work at Ole Miss and the thesis and dissertation on Faulkner—an excerpt of which had just recently been published in the *Southern Review*. I inquired about his collecting; he told me that he started to collect Faulkner as an undergraduate at Yale University twenty years earlier and had never stopped, though there had been an occasional hiatus. Then he excused himself and left the room. When he returned, he held a large safe-deposit box, a yard long and a foot deep. He placed it on the table, opened it, reached inside, and lifted an object delicately wrapped in soft, white tissue paper. Even before he unwrapped it, I knew it was a book, and I was fairly positive it would be a book by Faulkner. But I was still surprised when he removed the wrapping and laid the book before me on the table. It was a first edition of *The Sound and the Fury*. L.D. opened the book to the title page, on which I saw in small, meticulous handwriting, "William Faulkner / 30 Oct 1929." I had never seen a first edition of Faulkner's famous novel, much less a signed one, having used only the Modern Library reprint in my reading and research.

For the next two hours I sat at that table as L.D. retrieved box after box of items from the bank vault and displayed his treasures for me to see. There were first editions, with original dust jackets, of all of Faulkner's novels. There was a copy of the book that I later learned is the item most prized by Faulkner collectors—his first published book, a collection of poems entitled *The Marble Faun*. There were original manuscripts in Faulkner's neat, miniscule hand; burned fragments that had survived a 1942 house fire; manuscripts typed in Faulkner's two-finger, error-prone manner; as well as artwork, letters, photographs, wills, movie contracts, and other biographical documents. Having studied Faulkner for twenty years, I was quite familiar with the scholarly work on Faulkner. And I knew that I was looking at a number of artifacts that not even the most informed and celebrated Faulkner scholars had ever seen—or even knew existed. It was a heady experience. While a graduate student at Ole Miss, I had heard a visiting speaker, Professor C. Colleer Abbott, describe his discovery of some significant James Boswell papers in Malahide Castle in Scotland in 1936. The Mercantile Bank in Farmington, Missouri, was certainly no castle, but I felt I now knew something, albeit on a smaller scale, of the surprise and joy that Professor Abbott had experienced.

L.D. began his pursuit as a student at Yale, when he would visit Henry Wenning's bookstore near the campus and admire the signed editions he saw there. Initially L.D. collected books by a number of modern authors—Hemingway, Lewis, Frost, and others. However, while reading Faulkner in a seminar taught by R.W.B. Lewis, L.D. fell in love with Faulkner's magnificent prose and decided to make Faulkner the focus of his collecting passion. To fund that passion, L.D. would sometimes write home requesting money to buy books. His father later told me, "I couldn't believe how much money Yale students had to spend on textbooks."

At some point in our early discussions, I ventured to ask L.D. what he intended to do with the collection he was amassing. He wasn't sure, he responded; he had spent his efforts on locating and gathering the materials, and, beyond the sheer joy of acquiring the artifacts, he hadn't thought much about any ultimate purpose for the labor. I suggested that he consider mounting an exhibit of his collection's highlights on the Southeast Missouri State University campus. At Yale, L.D. had exhibited a small number of his books in a competition for amateur book collectors (he was awarded a prize in the contest), and later, as a graduate student at Washington University in St. Louis, he had mounted another small exhibit of Faulkner first editions. However, those exhibits had been years earlier, and his collection was now infinitely larger and more varied. So, yes, L.D. consented, it might be time to have a coming-out party for the Louis Daniel Brodsky Collection of William Faulkner Materials. We even joked about our possible scholarly collaboration beyond the exhibit: he had this marvelous Faulkner collection and I knew how to write a footnote.

Not long after our initial meetings, I invited a delegation from Southeast to accompany me to Farmington to discuss with L.D. plans for our proposed exhibit of his collection in our University Museum. Fred Goodwin, dean of the College of Humanities; Henry Sessoms, chairman of the English Department; M.G. Lorberg, a speech professor and board member of the Missouri Committee for the Humanities; and I were the university representatives. We met with L.D. in an upstairs conference room at the Mercantile Bank. Since none of my companions had previously met L.D., I had asked him to present an overview of his collection and share with the group his ideas about the organization and execution of an exhibit. The meeting went extremely well, with unanimous and enthusiastic expressions of interest in our proposal—but one development in the course of the discussion left our committee surprised, a bit puzzled, and amused.

Everyone who knew L.D. Brodsky will recall him as articulate, passionate, persuasive, and sometimes obsessively single minded. L.D. and I had already agreed on the idea of an exhibit, but we knew we would need the support of university administrators to make it happen. So, on this day, recognizing that he was speaking primarily to a group of non-Faulknerians, L.D. brought his entire rhetorical arsenal to the table. He described his collection, its provenance, its significance, and the national publicity the exhibit would bring to the university. As we say in sports, he had brought his A-game; he was in the zone.

L.D. was well into his presentation when a woman, obviously upset and distraught, came to the door and requested to speak with him. L.D. went to meet her, she whispered something to him, and they immediately headed down the stairs together, with no word of explanation to the rest of us. A few minutes later, L.D. returned to the conference room and resumed his presentation, again with no apology or explanation. Fred Goodwin, in telling the story later, insisted that L.D. picked up in the middle of a sentence, like a tape recorder that had been turned off and then, a short while later, back on.

After our meeting concluded, we all headed downstairs. As we reached the lower level we saw a couple of EMTs scurrying about and the swirling light of an ambulance through the open front door. In one of the offices we could see a man lying on the floor, connected to emergency equipment, and being attended by another EMT. Once outside, we asked L.D. if the man was someone he knew. Yes, L.D. said, he was a well-known businessman in town, and he had had a heart attack. The bank teller had come to secure L.D.'s assistance while they waited for the ambulance to arrive. "He's alive," L.D. assured us, "and they think he'll be okay." With that, we all headed to lunch.

Driving back to Cape Girardeau that afternoon, we all laughed about L.D.'s ability to maintain his composure and continue with his presentation despite the unexpected and near-tragic interruption. Henry Sessoms, the English professor, remarked, "He certainly knows how to stay on topic."

23

The first major exhibit of the Brodsky Faulkner collection, "William Faulkner: A Perspective from the Brodsky Collection," was presented in the Southeast Missouri State University Museum from October 2 to December 13, 1979. Dean Goodwin had not only secured the endorsement of the upper administration but had also arranged for a publication subsidy that would enable the University Press of Virginia to publish a hardbound catalog of the collection in conjunction with the exhibit. M.G. Lorberg persuaded the Missouri Committee for the Humanities to provide a grant to support the exhibit. Jim Parker, the director of the museum and also an artist with a keen aesthetic taste, displayed the materials beautifully.

Just a week before the exhibit opened, however, it looked like it might not open at all. L.D. was becoming more and more nervous about publicly displaying the materials, security being a huge concern; moreover, he and Parker were also having some disagreements about the handling of the treasures. Parker, a self-assured curator who had mounted exhibits for the Goldwater family when he worked in Arizona, had his own ideas about how to best display the books and manuscripts, and his ideas didn't always correspond with L.D.'s. At times it seemed the irresistible force had met the immovable object. It fell to Dean Goodwin and me to serve as peacemakers. Later Fred told me that he thought he and I should be nominated for the Nobel Peace Prize.

There's another Jim Parker story connected to the exhibit. Twenty-five hundred copies of an exquisite exhibit booklet were printed to hand out to viewers of the exhibit, but when area high school students came to view the items, as they did in great numbers, Jim would stand at the door as they exited and ask them to return the booklet if they had no use for it. Three months later, after the exhibit was dismounted, Jim called me to say there were some booklets left over and I could pick them up at my leisure. I said, "Thanks. I'll walk over there after class." He replied, "You'd better bring your car." When I arrived at the Museum, he pointed to a stack of boxes that contained several hundred of the remaindered (and reclaimed) booklets. Over the succeeding years, L.D. and I gave some of those copies to our friends, and I passed others out to visitors to the Brodsky Collection. These days I frequently see copies offered for sale on eBay and used book websites. And there are still a few leftover copies stacked in a storage room in the Center for Faulkner Studies.

In conjunction with the exhibit, L.D. and I had decided that a series of Faulkner lectures, some of which would be based on the materials being exhibited, would be a useful complement. I enlisted my former Faulkner professors, Thomas Daniel Young and John Pilkington, to address Faulkner's place in American literature. Jay Martin, a noted literary scholar and the director of a National Endowment for the Humanities seminar in which I had recently participated, spoke on Faulkner's relationship to Phil Stone and other male mentors. Henry Sessoms discussed the Phil Stone letters in L.D.'s collection. I analyzed the influence of Faulkner's great-grandfather, Colonel W.C. Falkner, on Faulkner's fiction; and L.D. concluded the series by talking about his collection and how he had succeeded in putting it together.

All in all, the exhibit and the accompanying lectures were a huge success. The *St. Louis Post-Dispatch* printed a full-page story on the exhibit, and notices appeared in the *New York Times*, the *Los Angeles Times*, and other prominent newspapers. Hundreds of people attended the exhibit and lectures, some coming from as far away as Chicago and New York. We received calls from Faulkner scholars who wanted to use the collection—and from individuals who wanted to sell to L.D. the Faulkner materials they had in their possession. "You blew my cover," L.D. told me, laughing. His early anxiety had subsided, and now he was clearly pleased with the public reception of his collection.

One Faulkner scholar who attended the exhibit—and took copious notes from the displayed materials for use in her next book—asked me at one point, "How did a school like this get this kind of an exhibit?" L.D.'s wife, Jan, who overheard the conversation, took the question as an insult and later told me I should have responded to it as such. I had simply laughed off the question and answered, quoting the old Avis ad, "We try harder." Over time, especially in the early years of our collaboration, that phrase would become something of a mantra for L.D. and me as we labored to promote the collection and bring to it the recognition and prominence it deserved.

COLLABORATION

The success of that 1979 exhibit—and the sheer joy and excitement that L.D. and I shared over the year and a half we spent in designing it and producing both the softbound catalog and the hardcover book that accompanied it—led us to explore additional ways that we might collaborate on projects relating to the collection. Fortunately, by this time we had an important ally and supporter who could advise us. Fredson Bowers was an emeritus English professor at the University of Virginia who, during his active career, had become known in literary circles as "the father of textual editing," and, in his retirement, was serving as the founding editor of *Studies in Bibliography*, the foremost periodical in the area of textual criticism. Dr. Bowers had not only secured the co-sponsorship of the Bibliographical Society of the University of Virginia (in cooperation with Southeast Missouri State University) for our *Selections from the William Faulkner Collection of Louis Daniel Brodsky: A Descriptive Catalogue* but also personally handled our negotiations with Jill Faulkner Summers, Faulkner's daughter and literary executrix, for permission to exhibit and publish some of her father's works.

Mrs. Summers shared many character traits with her father, one of which was her procrastination (and sometimes downright refusal) in answering her mail. L.D. had written her early on, requesting her permission and endorsement for our projects. After several weeks passed, however, with no response, L.D. explained the problem to Dr. Bowers, who graciously offered to hand-deliver a copy of the agreement to Mrs. Summers and secure her signature. This he did, allowing our plans to move forward.

Since we had already created something of a partnership with Dr. Bowers, it seemed to us that a logical next step would be to offer him a series of articles based on materials in the Brodsky Collection for possible publication in *Studies in Bibliography*. Dr. Bowers enthusiastically endorsed this proposal, and over the next three years, he accepted and published a number of articles that L.D. and I submitted, both individually and as co-authors. Together we authored an essay on Faulkner's first published poem, "*L'Apres Midi d'un Faune*"; L.D. published essays on another Faulkner poem, "A Dead Dancer," and one of Faulkner's finest short stories, "Wash"; and I published an essay on the contents of Faulkner's 1940 Last Will and Testament. L.D. also allowed Bowers to publish a manuscript from the Brodsky Collection, remarks Faulkner made in 1961 in Caracas, Venezuela, upon his receiving the Order of Andrés Bello award from the Venezuelan government.

With our work on the exhibit, the first book, and now several articles, my collaboration with L.D. was well established, though neither of us could have guessed that it would continue for more than three decades. Yet it very nearly did not.

Just as L.D. had previously been nervous about the public exhibit of his materials, he was now becoming increasingly anxious about the publication of some of those materials. In letters to me, he expressed concern that I was getting too deeply into the materials, conducting research that he eventually hoped to do for himself. He also expressed his fear that publishing the unique Faulkner materials in the collection might devalue their monetary worth.

By now I had become acutely aware of two opposing desires that drove L.D. in his Faulkner collecting. On the one hand, as demonstrated by the satisfaction and excitement he had experienced with the exhibit and our initial publications, he sincerely wanted to share his collection with others and to use it for the furtherance of Faulkner studies. On the other hand, he was, after all, an expert book collector, one of the best, and thus an individual who was always keenly conscious of the business side of collecting and who felt compelled to jealously guard his investment in the materials.

In the years following, I would find myself more and more fascinated, and impressed, as I watched L.D. deal with these conflicting emotions. If in the early years of our collaboration the business side of L.D. sometimes seemed to trump his scholarly side, by the middle and later years he became less and less concerned with collecting as a financial enterprise, and more and more committed to promoting and contributing to Faulkner scholarship. Watching L.D.'s growth and development in this regard proved to be one of the genuine satisfactions of our years together.

In one of the letters expressing his reservations about our ongoing collaboration, L.D. asked me to return the materials I was then working on and to sign an enclosed statement (his business side again) verifying that I would not make and retain any copies of said materials. I should add that this was the only time in all our years of collaboration that L.D. ever made such a request of me. I returned the materials, as requested, but I refused to sign the statement. I explained that I had not kept any copies, but he would have to take my word that such was the case. Our relationship from the beginning had been based on mutual trust, and I saw no reason to change that.

Believing at this point that our collaboration had come to an end, I turned to other matters, including an essay on Robert Frost that I had long considered writing. However, several weeks later I received a letter from Fredson Bowers, accompanied by another essay that L.D. had submitted to *Studies in Bibliography*. Bowers explained that he could not publish the essay in its current form and asked if I could assist L.D. in revising it into an acceptable essay. I returned the essay to Bowers, noting that I was no longer L.D.'s collaborator.

A few more weeks passed, and then one day my phone rang. It was L.D., saying he had reconsidered his decision about my involvement with his collection and inviting me to resume our collaboration. I gladly accepted the invitation, and two days later I received from L.D. a copy of the essay that Bowers had previously shared with me, with L.D.'s cover letter requesting my assistance in revising it.

I never learned what, if anything, passed between Bowers and L.D. on this matter. I proceeded to assist L.D. with the revision, and the essay was subsequently published in *Studies in Bibliography*. After a hiatus of several months, Brodsky and Hamblin were back in business. My Frost essay was back on hold.

Like our collaboration, L.D.'s Faulkner collection was beginning to formulate a life of its own, building momentum as it made its way into the world. L.D. and I both began to receive inquiries from scholars, graduate students engaged in Faulkner research, and even general readers who were excited to have more information on one of their favorite authors. All had questions about what other materials were in the collection and how they might be accessed. Since the exhibit and Virginia book had featured only highlights from the collection, clearly there was a need for a more comprehensive listing of the materials. Moreover, since the collection was still in private hands, and was a work-in-progress at that, there was no easy way for scholars to be granted access to the materials. The conference room at the Mercantile Bank in Farmington could not accommodate a host of visitors! Additionally, L.D.'s business enterprises—helping oversee a clothing factory in Farmington that employed more than three hundred workers, as well as managing seven retail stores in three states—simply didn't allow him (to paraphrase a famous Faulkner quote) to be at the beck and call of anybody with a postage stamp or a telephone.

Thus we needed a strategy for the dissemination of the materials in the collection. We settled on a plan that would include more journal articles, additional exhibits of the materials, periodic lectures at conferences and on university campuses, and, most importantly, a series of books that would present the unpublished manuscripts and documents in the collection.

Three other individuals crucial to our work at this stage now entered the picture: William Ferris, the founding director of the Center for the Study of Southern Culture at the University of Mississippi; Ann J. Abadie, the assistant director of the Center; and Barney McKee, the director of the University Press of Mississippi in Jackson. The Center agreed to sponsor, and the Press to publish, a multi-volume *Faulkner: A Comprehensive Guide to the Brodsky Collection*. The initial plans called for the publication of three volumes: a comprehensive catalog of the materials; a separate volume of letters by, to, or about Faulkner; and a book including the manuscripts and documents. However, after the appearance of the first two volumes in the series, in 1982 and 1984 respectively, L.D. acquired the Warner Bros. movie scripts authored or co-authored by Faulkner, and a decision was made to incorporate some of those into the *Comprehensive Guide* series. Thus, Volumes III and IV became, respectively, *The De Gaulle Story* (1984) and *Battle Cry* (1985), with *Manuscripts and Documents* being postponed until Volume V (1988). Additionally, two other books of Faulkner movie scripts were issued as supplements to the series: *Country Lawyer, and Other Stories for the Screen* (1987) and *Stallion Road* (1989). These volumes brought to eight the total number of books that L.D. and I produced from his marvelous collection. L.D. added a ninth book on his own, a collection of his independent essays and lectures on Faulkner. Titled *William Faulkner: Life Glimpses*, it was published by the University of Texas at Austin (1990). When I received my complimentary copy of that book, I was pleasantly surprised—and touched—to see myself included among the list of dedicatees, along with L.D.'s parents, wife, and children.

For the first six years of my collaboration with L.D., I drove to

29

Farmington and St. Louis, typically once or twice a month (and more often when a project was nearing completion), to work with him on the materials—in Farmington at the Mercantile Bank and in his home on West Columbia Street, and in St. Louis at his parents' home on Litzinger Road in Clayton. Items from the collection were housed at each of those locations. Occasionally, also, L.D. would travel to Cape Girardeau and stay overnight with Kaye and me at our house at 1557 Price Drive.

L.D. and I both enjoyed these overnight visits. I especially enjoyed working in his parents' home in Clayton. L.D.'s mother, Charlotte, was always a gracious hostess, and his father, Saul, encouraged and supported our work. On occasion he would interrupt us and say, "You boys are working too hard; come on, let's get some lunch." Another time he took us to the local Jewish synagogue to show us a series of paintings depicting the Creation that he and his wife had donated. I also enjoyed getting to know Bertha Riley, the Brodskys' housekeeper, an African American woman who was a native of Mississippi. Bertha and I had many interesting conversations about our native state.

On his trips to Cape Girardeau, L.D. frequently visited and sometimes guest-lectured in my classes—not only on Faulkner but also on poetry, writing, and other topics. During the years he lived in Farmington, L.D. was an adjunct instructor at Mineral Area Community College in Flat River (now Park Hills), so he was quite comfortable and adept in the classroom setting. My students always welcomed his visits.

Our wives, however, I'm quite sure, were not always as thrilled as we about our collaboration. L.D. and Jan were the parents of two young children, and, though Jan always treated me with the utmost civility and respect, I'm sure there were times when she found my frequent trips to Farmington to be an intrusion upon their family life. Similarly, Kaye sometimes felt that my work with L.D. interfered with our family activities. Once when L.D. and I were conversing on the deck at our home on Price Drive, Kaye, feeling neglected again, said, not altogether joking, "I'm going to find me a man who doesn't care anything about Faulkner." The topic of our conversation quickly changed.

In 1984, on one of his visits to our campus, I escorted L.D. into our library's Rare Book Room, which at that time was used exclusively to display the Charles Harrison collection of rare books. Harrison, a Cape Girardeau businessman and an avid book collector, had willed his book collection to Southeast upon his death in 1944. The collection contains over eight hundred titles, illustrating the history of book publishing from the thirteenth to the early twentieth century. In 1968, when the university constructed a new library, the Harrison family established and furnished the Rare Book Room, and Harrison's books were displayed in beautiful, glass-encased cabinets that lined the back wall. Open shelves lined the side walls, but these shelves remained empty, as no additional collections had been placed in the room. To my knowledge, only one Southeast professor had ever used the Harrison Collection for research, and the room was only occasionally opened to students and visitors. Most people on campus knew the room only as the library room that was usually locked.

Knowing that L.D. would appreciate seeing the results achieved by a fellow bibliophile and collector, I escorted him into the room and watched as he closely examined first editions of almost all of Mark Twain's novels, a first edition of *Moby Dick*, a complete set of the periodicals that first published Dickens's *David Copperfield*, an early edition containing color prints of Audubon's bird drawings, a copy of Edgar Lee Masters' *Spoon River Anthology* with a laid-in manuscript in the poet's own hand, and many more rare collectibles.

Admiring the impressive books, the dark mahogany shelves and cases, and the ornate furniture, L.D. said, "I'd love to have a room like this for my collection."

Laughing and pointing to the empty shelves, I replied, "You may use this one."

Not long afterward, L.D. asked me to check with the Southeast administrators to see if they would be amenable to the deposit of the Brodsky Collection in the Rare Book Room. L.D. would retain ownership of the collection, but the university would warehouse it for him and be allowed to mount exhibits and present other programs organized around the collection. Placement of the materials at Southeast would also facilitate my work with the collection—and allow L.D., for the first time, to bring the collection together in one location.

James Zink, then director of Kent Library, enthusiastically supported this proposal, in part because he saw it as an opportunity to secure needed improvements in the Rare Book Room. The multi-million dollar Harrison Collection had been deposited in the Rare Book Room for sixteen years—without the benefit of a climate-controlled environment or even a security system. The arrival of the Brodsky Collection, more than doubling the value of the contents of the room, would require these additions. Thus, as would prove to be the case numerous times in coming years, the Brodsky Collection became a catalyst for other campus improvements and achievements.

Ultimately the decision to allow the Brodsky Collection to be moved into the Rare Book Room under the custody of the university lay with the school's president, Bill W. Stacy, and provost, Leslie Cochran. And they too, like Zink, had interests and goals quite beyond the promotion of Faulkner studies. In the mid-'80s and early '90s, Southeast was trying to break out of its provincial identity to achieve "national prominence." A part of that strategy was to enhance the academic reputation of the school by raising entrance requirements for students and standards of tenure and promotion for faculty. The general education program was significantly revised, moving from a two-year, disconnected, cafeteria-style offering of introductory courses in various disciplines to a unified, objectives-based program (designated "University Studies") spread over four years and including such features as team teaching and senior-level capstone seminars. In athletics, the university moved from Division II of the NCAA to the more prestigious (and expensive) Division I. An ongoing and developing relationship with one of the world's great Faulkner collections would be another useful component in a larger overall strategy to enhance the status and image of the university.

Once the decision had been made to house the Brodsky Collection in the Rare Book Room, preparations in the room were implemented. Climate-control and security systems were installed, and, for added security, doors with locks were added to the open shelves that would hold L.D.'s books. As these improvements were being planned, I asked L.D. how many of the shelves would be needed to hold his collection. He looked at the open shelves, thought for a moment, and then, pointing to the west side of the room, said, "About half of that wall." He had never seen the entire collection in one place, so he was offering his best estimate.

He and I were both surprised when we started moving the materials from Farmington and St. Louis into the Rare Book Room. Not only did the collection fill the entire west wall of the room and curve around the corner to fill one cabinet of the north wall and several shelves on the east wall, but also an additional credenza had to be installed to hold the remaining overflow. In sheer volume, the collection was far larger than even L.D. himself suspected.

After the collection was moved into the Rare Book Room, my work, of course, became much easier. While my colleagues were traveling to libraries and research centers across the country (and Max Cordonnier, the William Blake scholar, and Dan Straubel, the Melville scholar, to England) to conduct their research, I had only to climb the hill from the Grauel Building to Kent Library to do my work. Now it was L.D. who was on the road, driving more frequently to Cape Girardeau, since our working office had shifted from Farmington and St. Louis to the Rare Book Room on the Southeast campus. But the work continued apace.

The exhibits that we worked on during those years proved especially rewarding. Selecting the materials to be exhibited, planning and writing the exhibit catalogs, and arranging the displays were not only ways of enhancing our (and the viewers') study of Faulkner but also of developing our mutual respect and friendship. As a collector, L.D. enjoyed the physical act of handling and examining the books, manuscripts, and documents, each one with its own story of origin, provenance, and acquisition. As a Faulkner scholar, I learned from L.D. and his collection more and more about Faulkner's life and career. If T.D. Young and John Pilkington had been the first two teachers to lead me through Faulkner's Yoknapatawpha, L.D. Brodsky was now proving to be the third.

Two 1983 exhibits focused on L.D.'s work as a collector—"Brodsky: The Evolution of a Faulkner Collector/Scholar," mounted at the University of Tulsa at the invitation of noted Faulkner scholar James Watson, a professor at that school; and "Brodsky: A Faulkner Collector/Scholar at Work," displayed at the University of Mississippi in conjunction with the annual Faulkner and Yoknapatawpha Conference. In 1984, following L.D.'s acquisition of the screenplays Faulkner wrote for Warner Bros. Studio, we mounted "Faulkner and Hollywood: A Retrospective from the Brodsky Collection" in Kent Library. Presented in conjunction with the annual meeting of the Missouri Philological Association, which was hosted by our English department on the Southeast campus, this exhibit celebrated the deposit of the Brodsky Collection in our Rare Book Room. Its broader significance was that it publicized an area of Faulkner's creativity—his movie work—that is, even today, too frequently ignored by Faulkner scholars. On another occasion, we displayed a large number of photographs from the Brodsky Collection.

One exhibit gave both L.D. and me particular satisfaction. From time to time over the years as we worked on the various exhibits, I had suggested to L.D. that at some point he should select and exhibit his favorite items from the collection, a kind of "Greatest Hits" album. He agreed and, in 1989, when we made the trip to Ann Arbor, Michigan, to acquire the Joseph Blotner papers (the research files that Blotner compiled in writing his monumental biography of Faulkner), we created that exhibit en route. As L.D. drove, he would identify a favorite item and make a brief comment about it. I made a list of the items and wrote down his comments. By the time we arrived back in St. Louis, I had a list of one hundred items divided into various categories—books, manuscripts, letters, art work, movie scripts, photographs, biographical documents—along with L.D.'s comments about how he acquired the item or why he liked it or what its significance was. The next week I typed up the list, and we had our next exhibit—"The Collector's 101 Favorites"—which we mounted in the Rare Book Room in 1989 to celebrate the creation of Southeast's Center for Faulkner Studies. Joseph Blotner, Faulkner's biographer, opened the exhibit with a lecture on Faulkner and the significance of the Brodsky collection. That exhibit catalog has now had a life well beyond the exhibit itself, going through three separate printings and also being disseminated on the internet.

The 101st item of the title was one that L.D. had not yet placed in the collection at Southeast. It was Faulkner's "Pocket Ben" watch that Faulkner used on his sailboat on Sardis Lake. Faulkner had signed the back of the watch with a sharp stylus: "W. Faulkner / Ring Dove." L.D.'s comment on the watch was "one to grow on." For years the watch lay beside his typewriter as he wrote. In 2013, he finally donated the watch to Southeast, adding it to the rest of his Faulkner collection.

In addition to creating our own exhibits, we lent materials from the collection for exhibit elsewhere. The Library of Congress borrowed Faulkner's hand-drawn map of his fictional Yoknapatawpha to include in a display of literary maps. The Japanese William Faulkner Society borrowed photographs from the Brodsky Collection for an exhibit at its annual conference. The Herbert Hoover Presidential Library and Museum, located in West Branch, Iowa, borrowed materials for one of its exhibits. The University of Mississippi exhibited items relating to Faulkner's close friendship with his Random House editor, Saxe Commins.

My Faulkner collaboration with L.D. Brodsky lasted for thirty-six years, and in all that time we never executed any type of formal contract. Only twice in our years together was such an arrangement even considered. The first time, discussed above, was when L.D. temporarily ended our collaboration and asked me to sign a statement testifying that I was returning to him all materials I had on loan. As I noted, I refused to sign the statement, and, to his credit and my great relief, L.D. never again asked me to sign any type of formal agreement.

The second time presented to me a temptation that I found very hard to resist. To my knowledge, L.D.'s only real complaint against me over the years was my occasional difficulty in meeting a publishing deadline. From time to time I would have to remind him that I worked at a teaching institution, not a research institution, and that my teaching duties would always have to take precedence over my Faulkner research. As a result, sometimes our joint projects progressed at a slower rate than L.D. would have preferred.

On one such occasion, with the University Press of Mississippi objecting to our delay in completing one volume in the *Comprehensive Guide* series, L.D. offered to pay me the equivalent of my summer salary at Southeast, thus relieving me of my teaching duties and allowing me to work full time on the book. It was an attractive and generous proposal, but after due consideration, I declined the offer. In retrospect I see it as one of the wisest decisions I ever made in my working with L.D. The challenges and difficulties of collaboration were sufficient enough without the added pressure of legal contracts and business arrangements. And (perhaps my ego came into play here) I was unwilling to become an "employee" of L.D. Brodsky, even for a short period of time and for a good cause.

Thus, our partnership, from the beginning to the end, remained a "handshake" agreement, based on mutual friendship and trust, and ultimately neither of us would have wanted it any other way. At the outset we agreed that we would work together only so long as it continued to be fun, and if and when it ceased to be fun, either of us could walk away. But that day never came.

There is one other point I would like to emphasize about our collaboration. I was already a full professor when I met L.D. in 1978, so my publications related to the Brodsky Collection (considerable in number by now) contributed nothing to my advancement in academic rank. I have always eschewed the "publish or perish" mentality that governs many institutions of higher education (though, thankfully, not Southeast), and one of my principal points of personal pride has been that all of my work on the Brodsky Collection came after I had already been advanced by my institution to the highest professorial rank. To be sure, my Faulkner work has brought me many rewards over the years, financial and otherwise, but I am happy to say that none of it has been demanded or required.

Similarly, on his side of the ledger, L.D. considered himself primarily a poet, secondarily a businessman, and only thirdly a Faulkner collector. Moreover, unlike those collectors who simply want to hoard collectibles or use them as an investment, L.D.'s collecting was primarily motivated by his sheer love for Faulkner's writings and his desire to promote a broader interest in and admiration for those writings.

Truly, then, for each of us, working on the Louis Daniel Brodsky Collection of William Faulkner Materials was, from beginning to end, a labor of love.

Sleuthsayer

Book collectors are the unsung heroes in literary studies. In the hierarchy of this profession, authors, as of course they should be, are at the top of the apex, since they are the artists who create the works without which there would be no readers and no critics. Next are the editors and publishers who present an author's work to the general public. Then come the reviewers and critics who assist readers in understanding and interpreting an author's works. Good criticism is itself an art form, and while a good critic cannot make a bad author into a good one, an intelligent and insightful critic can greatly elucidate and enhance any author's stature. William Faulkner has benefitted immensely from the work of a host of outstanding critics: Malcolm Cowley, Robert Penn Warren, Jean Paul Sartre, Maurice Coindreau, Richard P. Adams, Carvel Collins, Cleanth Brooks, Hyatt Waggoner, Michael Millgate, and Olga Vickery, to name only a few of the ones who were instrumental in establishing Faulkner's reputation as a major author.

There is one type of critic who, though crucial—indeed, indispensable—to literary studies, is frequently overlooked by the reading public. These are the textual critics, the ones who work diligently to give readers the texts we read. They pore over manuscripts and typescripts, decipher difficult handwriting and marginalia, interpret revisions, and collate variant passages in order to produce the closest thing possible to the exact text that the author wants the reader to read. Here again, Faulkner has been extremely fortunate in his critics: James B. Meriwether, Noel Polk, Thomas McHaney, Judith Sensibar, Bruce Kawin, and Sarah Gleeson-White, among others, have labored long and hard to provide definitive texts of Faulkner's novels, stories, poems, and movie scripts.

There is still one more person involved in the field of literary production, one who is forgotten or ignored even more than the textual critic. This is the collector. Sometimes he is the one who makes the work of a textual critic possible, since it is he who acquires, collects, and preserves artifacts that otherwise might have been irretrievably lost. It might be a book, an early draft of a manuscript, a diary or journal, or a letter, or other personal document that the collector salvages from the dust bins of history. Whether collectors be private individuals, like Louis Daniel Brodsky, or archivists working for museums or libraries or institutions, their work is indispensable to the researchers and critics and, through them, the readers.

All serious Faulkner scholars know the invaluable contributions that collectors have made to Faulkner studies. Linton Massey's private collection became the cornerstone of the University of Virginia's massive Faulkner holdings. His *Man Working, 1919-1962, William Faulkner* is both a tribute to and a how-to manual for all book collectors. William Wisdom's Faulkner collection is now housed at Tulane, the Webb family's at the University of Mississippi, and Toby Holtzman's at the University of Michigan. And L.D. Brodsky's collection went to Southeast Missouri State University, becoming the catalyst for the creation of the Center for Faulkner Studies in 1989. William Boozer and Carl Petersen also built significant Faulkner collections and graciously opened their holdings to many scholars; unfortunately, those collections were not acquired intact by an institution and as a result have been scattered among numerous buyers.

Brodsky, Petersen, and Boozer were contemporaries and friendly rivals in their acquisition of Faulkner materials. All three of them frequently attended the annual Faulkner and Yoknapatawpha Conference in Oxford. Their rivalry is mirrored in the following conversation I overheard at one of those conferences.

In 1983, in conjunction with that year's conference, the Faulkner plaque now displayed on the wall of the Layayette County courthouse was dedicated and unveiled. Many of us who attended the conference that year, including the three collectors, gathered on the lawn of the courthouse to observe the ceremony. The speaker for the event was Dr. Chester McLarty, Faulkner's personal physician and close friend. When McLarty completed his remarks, one member of the audience turned to another and jokingly commented, "I wonder which collector will get the manuscript of Dr. McLarty's remarks."

Overhearing the comment, Bill Boozer reached inside his coat pocket, pulled out some typewritten pages, and waved them about, laughing. His friend Chester had already given him an inscribed copy of the speech. Another bystander remarked, "What does that leave for Carl and L.D.?"

Someone else remarked, "Carl plans to come back after dark and take the plaque."

"And Brodsky?"

"He's waiting for Rowan Oak," I said.

L.D. uses a portmanteau word to describe the work of the collector. That word is "sleuthsayer," a hybrid term combining "sleuth," that is, a detective, with "soothsayer," or prophet. The collector, L.D. says, must, like the detective, uncover and utilize clues to locate artifacts, and he must possess a visionary sense of which author and which artifacts to collect. L.D. was wise to choose an author of such stature as Faulkner to collect, and he became expert at discovering and following clues that enabled him to develop his collection into world-class status.

In various essays and books, L.D. describes how he came to possess some of his favorite items in his collection. Initially, he acquired signed Faulkner books through book dealers, like Henry Wenning in New Haven and Margie Cohn in New York. But he quickly realized that he could never develop a comprehensive collection working merely through dealers and auctions. So he reached out to the two foremost Faulkner scholars of the 1950s and '60s, Carvel Collins and James B. Meriwether, for their advice and direction. Both provided invaluable assistance, pointing L.D. to sources they had uncovered as the first Faulkner scholars to conduct serious, detailed research on Faulkner's life and career.

When Joseph Blotner's massive biography of Faulkner appeared in 1974, L.D. used it as a guide, searching its pages for the names of Faulkner relatives, friends, and acquaintances who might still be in possession of Faulkner books, letters, or documents. His timing was perfect, since many of those items had by that time passed to second-generation holders who, in many cases, did not have the personal and sentimental attachment to the items that the original owners had. L.D. would contact those individuals, arrange to meet them and view the materials, and negotiate a price to acquire the artifacts. In more cases than not, given his power of persuasion and his (and his father's) bankroll, he was successful.

Over the next several years, L.D.'s work as "sleuthsayer" took him to all parts of the United States. In Sulphur Springs, West Virginia, he found Myrtle Ramey Demarest, who had been a childhood classmate of Faulkner in Oxford. Myrtle had married and left Oxford after high school, but she had followed her friend's writing career with interest, and she had a standing order on file with Mac Reed in Oxford for a signed copy of each Faulkner novel that was published. Book by book, Reed would secure Faulkner's inscription to Myrtle, then package and mail the book to her. Myrtle was now, these years later, living in a nursing home, but her daughter was in possession of her mother's Faulkner books.

It was these signed books that L.D. traveled to West Virginia to acquire, but what else he found was a serendipitous surprise. For Christmas in 1924, Myrtle had traveled back to Oxford to visit family, and during that visit Faulkner presented to her an inscribed sheaf of twelve carbon typescript poems, accompanied by a title page that states: "Mississippi Poems." Included in the group were seven poems that would subsequently be published in Faulkner's second and final volume of poems, *A Green Bough* (1933).

Additionally, Faulkner gave Myrtle ten pen-and-ink cartoons that he had drawn in 1913 for a high school yearbook that was never produced. These drawings include caricatures of the school principal, G.G. Hurst, and various faculty members, as well as cartoons that reflect an aversion (undoubtedly Faulkner's) to school and homework. The most interesting of the cartoons is one showing Miss Ella Wright, the history teacher, turning the handle of a machine labeled "Demerit Mill" and grinding out punishment for a fierce, ogre-like "A. Lincoln." Drawn in miniature, at Lincoln's feet and with his obvious approval, a large Union bully armed with a knife is attacking a small, unarmed Confederate. The caption on the drawing reads: "Them's my sentiments!" Almost certainly, those words—and the content of the drawing—reflect the way Miss Wright taught American history in the Oxford Graded School (that is, from a Confederate point of view), but they probably mirror the sixteen-year-old Billy Falkner's views as well.

In Sulphur Springs, after Brodsky had negotiated a price for Myrtle's books and was preparing to leave, his hostess pointed him to a box of old papers and said, "You're welcome to look through those things to see if there's anything else you'd like to have. They're headed to the trash dump."

The box contained the manuscript of "Mississippi Poems" and the high school cartoons.

In Tulsa, Oklahoma, L.D. visited Vance Broach, one of Faulkner's cousins who, like Faulkner, was a grand-nephew of Mrs. Alabama McLean, "Aunt 'Bama." Broach had inherited a number of Faulkner-related items from Mrs. McLean of Memphis, the last surviving daughter of the "Old Colonel," William C. Falkner. These materials included several typescript poems that Faulkner had presented to Aunt 'Bama, newspaper clippings about Faulkner that Mrs. McLean had collected and preserved over the years—and the handwritten ledger of the Ripley Railroad Company, founded by her father. The ledger, covering the years 1871–1873, contains entries written by both Colonel Falkner and his partner and eventual assassin, R.J. Thurmond.

Broach cherished these items he had from his great-aunt, but, as fate would have it, what he really desired to own was a copy of Faulkner's first book, *The Marble Faun*. By this time in his collecting, L.D. had managed to secure three copies of this rare book, so he traded one of those copies to Broach for the Aunt 'Bama materials. This was the first of numerous "swap-outs" that L.D. arranged in the course of building his collection.

In Tampa, Florida, L.D. acquired several Faulkner items from James Silver, former history professor at Ole Miss and a close friend of the Faulkners. An outspoken liberal who authored *Mississippi: The Closed Society* and the autobiographical *Running Scared: Silver in Mississippi*, Silver had left Ole Miss (before being fired) in 1965, in the wake of the school's integration crisis. He then taught for a few years at Notre Dame and subsequently finished out his teaching career at the University of South Florida.

Included in the nearly four hundred pages of materials L.D. acquired from Silver is a copy of the speech, "American Segregation and the World Crisis," that Faulkner made, at Silver's behest, at a meeting of the Southern Historical Society in Memphis in November 1955. A three-paragraph addendum to the speech that Faulkner typed and gave to Silver for inclusion in the published version of the speech reads in part: "We will not sit quietly by and see our native land, the South, not just Mississippi but all the South, wreck and ruin itself twice in less than a hundred years over the Negro question. We speak now against the day when our Southern people ... will say, 'Why didn't someone tell us this before? Tell us this in time?'"

Brodsky also acquired from Silver one of the most prized items in the Brodsky Collection—a copy of Albert Einstein's book, *Ideas and Opinions*, that Einstein had personally inscribed to Faulkner. The two men met in Princeton in 1954, and Einstein presented Faulkner with the book in the home of Saxe Commins, Faulkner's Random House editor. Einstein's inscription reads: "To Mr. Faulkner / (without obligo) / A. Einstein 54." A presentation copy signed by a Nobel Prize-winning physicist to a Nobel Prize-winning author is a book to be prized by any collector! This book, after being given to Faulkner in Princeton, made its way with Faulkner to Rowan Oak, and then, following Faulkner's death, was given to Silver by Estelle Faulkner. Silver carried the book with him to Indiana and Florida, and eventually Brodsky brought it from Florida to St. Louis and then to Cape Girardeau, for deposit in the Brodsky Collection.

In 1983, L.D. travelled to Hollywood to acquire some books from A.I. "Buzz" Bezzerides, a novelist and screenwriter with whom Faulkner had worked at Warner Bros. Studio in the early 1940s. Faulkner had actually boarded in Bezzerides's home for several weeks. Brodsky spent a week with Bezzerides in that same home, negotiating the purchase of the several novels that Faulkner had inscribed to Bezzerides, as well as conducting an interview of him that was subsequently published in the *Southern Review*.

On the last day of his visit, with only a couple of hours left before he was to catch his plane back to St. Louis, L.D. was given the run of the house and invited to look for other books that Bezzerides, now in his seventies, might have overlooked. In an old desk stored in the basement, L.D. found a thick folder identified on the cover as "The De Gaulle Story by William Faulkner." L.D. had previously obtained a set of the Warner Bros. screenplays authored by Faulkner, which included copies of several different versions of the De Gaulle script, so when he saw the blue folder at Bezzerides's, he knew what he was looking at. But when he opened and thumbed through this copy of the screenplay, he quickly noticed that it was different from the others he had seen. This one was not typed with the professional skill of those obviously prepared by the studio's secretarial pool, but in the amateurish, error-prone, strikeover-ridden manner that L.D. had come to recognize as Faulkner's own unskilled typing. Additionally, as he continued thumbing through the pages, he found Faulkner's handwritten corrections and interlineations scattered throughout. As he and I determined later when we prepared the De Gaulle materials for publication, what he had discovered was Faulkner's original script of *The De Gaulle Story*. Unknown to Bezzerides, Faulkner had left it behind when he walked out on Warner Bros. in 1945 and returned to Mississippi.

In 1989, I accompanied L.D. to Ann Arbor, Michigan, to examine the research files that Joseph Blotner had compiled in writing his monumental Faulkner biography. In those pre-computer days, Blotner had stored his notes and papers in manila folders and placed the folders into long, rectangular boxes that originally held egg cartons but now provided a perfect fit for the manila folders. There were eight or ten of these large boxes, as I recall, each one containing a hundred or more individual folders. Blotner had organized the results of his twenty-year research into three distinct categories: a straight chronology paralleling Faulkner's life; an alphabetical order of Faulkner's published work; and an alphabetical listing of the names of important personages, as well as Blotner's many correspondents.

L.D., Blotner, and I spent the entire day looking through the boxes and folders, breaking only for a lunch prepared for us by Blotner's beautiful and gracious wife, Yvonne. L.D. and Blotner had previously talked by telephone about a possible sale and acquisition, but, understandably, L.D. wanted to see the materials before he finalized the deal. It was late afternoon before the examination and discussion were concluded, at which point L.D. wrote a $30,000 personal check to Blotner and we loaded the heavy boxes into the back of L.D.'s station wagon.

Since we decided to wait until the next day to drive back to St. Louis, L.D. and I checked into a local motel for the night. It had been a long and tiring day, but L.D. was nervous about leaving the boxes in his station wagon overnight, so we moved the materials into the motel room with us. The next morning we had to load the boxes back into the station wagon. Actually, *I* had to. While I lugged box after box to the station wagon, L.D. sat on the end of the bed and watched one of his favorite television shows, *Sesame Street*. Not until Big Bird had done his thing and the show had ended could we begin our drive back home.

In 2001, L.D. acquired from Victoria ("Vicky") Fielden Black the copy of "The Wishing Tree" that Faulkner hand produced and presented to Vicky's mother, Victoria ("Cho Cho") Franklin, as a birthday gift in 1927. Faulkner had made a typescript copy of the story, stapled the pages together, and bound them in a cardboard cover. He then produced a watercolor drawing on the front cover and affixed the title in his personal artistic script. On the front flyleaf he identified the book as a "first printing, only impression," and he inscribed the book: "For his dear friend Victoria on her eighth birthday Bill he made this Book."

Faulkner would later present handmade copies of this story to three other children: later that same year to Dr. Calvin Brown's daughter Margaret, who was dying of leukemia, and, in 1948, to Ruth Ford's daughter Shelley and Phil Stone's son Philip. But Cho-Cho's copy has a unique significance, since it was a gift of courtship to Cho-Cho's mother as much as a present to a young child. In 1927, Estelle Franklin separated from her husband, Cornell Franklin, in Shanghai, and returned to Oxford with her two children, Victoria and Malcolm. Faulkner quickly resumed his courtship with Estelle, and, following her divorce from Franklin, Faulkner and his childhood sweetheart, whom he had lost for a time to another man, were married in 1929.

Not often, but occasionally, L.D. had to resort to subterfuge to acquire certain materials. One day I received a call from Hubert McAlexander, a friend and former graduate school classmate who was a professor of English at the University of Georgia. Did I know, Hubert inquired, that Jimmy Faulkner was shopping around a number of letters that Faulkner had written to his mother? No, I replied, I hadn't heard. "Well," Hubert said, "you might want to contact Jimmy."

When I called Jimmy to inquire about the letters, his reply was quite to the point: "I don't want Brodsky to have the letters." He didn't explain why, and I didn't ask. Rather, I tried another approach.

"Well, you know that Brodsky has transferred ownership of his collection to our university, so he doesn't own it any more. You'd be dealing with Southeast Missouri State University, not L.D. Brodsky."

Jimmy was still not persuaded, though he did agree not to sell the letters until he had called me and given us a chance to bid on them. However, time passed and he never called me back.

When it became clear that Jimmy was not going to let either L.D. or Southeast purchase the letters, L.D. contacted a New York book dealer with whom he had done business over the years. L.D. asked the dealer to contact Jimmy Faulkner and arrange to purchase the letters, after which the dealer would then sell the letters to L.D. And that's what happened.

At the next Faulkner conference I reminded Jimmy that he had never called me back about the letters and asked him if he still had them. "No," he said, "I sold them to a New York book dealer." I don't know if Jimmy ever learned that the letters are now a part of the Brodsky Collection.

Thus it continued. Item by item, year by year, using one approach or another, L.D. expanded his collection. In Osceola, Arkansas, he acquired materials from Phil "Moon" Mullen, former editor of the *Oxford Eagle*, who had been the first newspaperman to interview Faulkner following his winning of the Nobel Prize for Literature. In Montgomery, Alabama, L.D. obtained items from Emily Whitehurst Stone, the widow of Faulkner's lifelong friend and early mentor, Phil

Stone. In Princeton, New Jersey, he acquired items (including the typewriter Faulkner used to type portions of *A Fable*) from Dorothy Commins, the widow of Faulkner's Random House editor, Saxe Commins. In Greenville, Mississippi, he obtained materials from Ben Wasson, Faulkner's college classmate, good friend, and first literary agent. In Sherman, Connecticut, he purchased materials from Malcolm Cowley, editor of the influential *The Portable Faulkner*.

During his negotiations with Cowley, L.D. shared with me descriptions of the books, letters, and other items that he might be able to acquire. There was one book, though, that he probably would pass on: Cowley's copy of *Absalom, Absalom!*, since it had an entire chapter that had been razored out. Condition of a book is a primary concern of any collector, and few serious collectors would want a book with missing pages.

When L.D. shared with me his description of this particular book, I said to him, "You know why those pages are missing, don't you?" No, he said, he didn't know.

I explained that when Cowley was putting together his *Portable Faulkner*, he discovered that most of Faulkner's books were out of print and unavailable even in second-hand bookshops. Thus, to provide the typesetter with a copy of the chapter from *Absalom* that he wanted to include in the *Portable* (Chapter V, which Cowley published as "Wedding in the Rain"), he had to excise those pages from his own personal copy of the book. Once L.D. knew the history of the mutilation of the book, he was eager to acquire it. Seldom will damage to a book increase rather than diminish its appeal, but this was one of those occasions.

This was one of the very few times that I had any active involvement in L.D.'s collecting ventures. Another that I recall was during the initial exhibit of the Brodsky Collection at Southeast, when I received a phone call from an individual who had read a newspaper story about the exhibit. Mistaking me for the collector, he offered me some oil paintings done by Faulkner's mother, Maud. I quickly explained that I was not the collector, and I gave him contact information for L.D. The next time I visited L.D. in Farmington, he had some new acquisitions to show me—a number of oil paintings by Maud Falkner.

But these cases were exceptions, not the rule. My role in L.D.'s collecting was merely to cheer him on from the sidelines and watch him work his magic. The luckiest scholar in America, I had only to sit and wait until he delivered the next treasure to my very door.

SEMO Acquires the Collection

During the spring of 1988, L.D. asked me to set up an appointment with Bill Stacy, the president of Southeast Missouri State University. I did so, and the three of us met for a casual lunch in the University Center on campus. Early in that meeting L.D. said to Bill, "I want to talk with you about placing my Faulkner collection at Southeast." Having had no previous inkling that this topic was to be the purpose of the meeting, I was totally shocked by L.D.'s statement.

When L.D. and I initiated our collaboration on his Faulkner collection, I made two promises to him: 1) we will work together only as long as it is fun for both of us, and 2) no one at Southeast will ever ask you for your collection. I knew that a number of institutions were pursuing the collection, sometimes to L.D.'s great annoyance, and I didn't want Southeast added to that list. And we never were. In the ten years that L.D. and I had worked together, and even after the collection was already housed in our Rare Book Room, no one from Southeast had ever asked for the collection.

Another reason I was shocked by L.D.'s offer was that I knew he had been engaged in serious discussion over the past several months with the University of Mississippi to place his collection there. Actually, as I would learn only years later, this was L.D.'s second attempt to place his collection at Ole Miss. He had offered his collection to Ole Miss back in 1982. Then Chancellor Porter L. Fortune asked Grey Cole, head of the Ole Miss library, to negotiate with Brodsky the terms of the acquisition. In a letter to the chancellor dated October 6, 1982, Cole reported that the chances of a deal looked favorable, and he outlined the major points from his discussion with L.D. The asking price for the collection, which L.D. said had been appraised at $2.5 million, would be at least $750,000, which could be paid in one lump sum or over a period of 15–20 years. L.D. would also require the creation of a special library room to house and display the collection; Cole estimated that the cost of this provision would be around $50,000.

While Cole expressed his belief that the monetary arrangements could be met, especially if donors could be found to assist the university with the purchase price of the collection, he informed Chancellor Fortune that there might be problems with some of L.D.'s other requests. For example, L.D. wanted the future Faulkner room to be created to be named after him, even though it would also house Faulkner materials acquired from other donors. Additionally, L.D. requested sole scholarly control of the Brodsky Collection until such time as he and I had completed the projects we already had underway, principally the *Comprehensive Guide* series for the University Press of Mississippi. Finally, L.D. wanted Ole Miss to sponsor and publish two additional books that he expected to complete within the next two years: one, a volume of poems titled *Mistress Mississippi*, a companion volume to his earlier *Mississippi Vistas*; and two, a collection of his essays on the "hows and whys" of the building of his Faulkner collection.

For whatever reasons, these initial negotiations between L.D. and Ole Miss stalled, and Porter Fortune retired as Ole Miss chancellor in 1984. Shortly after his successor, Gerald Turner, was appointed, L.D. reopened his discussions about the collection with the new chancellor. Only at this point did I become aware of L.D.'s interest in placing the collection at Ole Miss. I was thrilled to learn that such was the case.

Behind the scenes, without L.D.'s knowledge, I encouraged Ole Miss's interest and even advised them on major points in their dealing with L.D. Since Southeast was not a Ph.D.-granting research institution, I never dreamed that L.D. would consider it as a repository of his collection. Moreover, quite naturally I much preferred my alma mater as a home for the materials over, say, Yale or Washington University, both of whom had expressed interest. Yale had even sent a representative to Cape Girardeau to talk with me about the Brodsky Collection.

For a number of reasons, Ole Miss was the logical place for the collection. It's located in Oxford, Faulkner's hometown; the university possesses a very fine Faulkner collection and also owns and operates Faulkner's home Rowan Oak; and the school's Center for the Study of Southern Culture was sponsor of the Brodsky and Hamblin books being published by the University Press of Mississippi. L.D. and I had been invited speakers at the annual Faulkner and Yoknapatawpha Conference, and L.D. had collaborated with Thomas Verich, head of Ole Miss's Special Collections, on an exhibit and related catalog for one of those conferences. It seemed to me at one point that Ole Miss had a virtual lock on acquiring the collection. And I was pleased with that prospect.

But things don't always happen as expected or planned.

Ole Miss, understandably, was hopeful that Brodsky would donate the collection to the university. But I knew that was not going to happen. While attending the 1987 Faulkner and Yoknapatawpha Conference, I arranged a meeting with Chancellor Turner. During that conversation I explained that while I felt L.D. would be willing to donate a major portion of the value of the collection, he would require some cash payment as part of the transaction.

Here was my reasoning, rightly or wrongly. Like most sons of highly successful fathers, L.D. always hungered for the approval of his father. Saul Brodsky, a self-made multi-millionaire, was a wonderful, caring individual, but as a tough-minded businessman, what he most valued was the bottom line. By contrast, what L.D. most valued was poetry and literature, and although his father tolerated the son's interests, he did not share or encourage them. Additionally, much of L.D.'s Faulkner collecting was being done on "company time," to say nothing of "company money," since he was pursuing his collecting activities at the same time that he was overseeing a factory and establishing and managing retail stores for his father's manufacturing company. Whether the result of conscious or unconscious guilt, or merely the desire to demonstrate to his father that Faulkner collecting could be as profitable as a business enterprise, it was crucial for L.D. to prove, perhaps to himself but even more to his father, that book collecting was not just an expensive hobby or, worse, a waste of time. Receiving a significant amount of money for the collection would presumably validate L.D.'s efforts—to himself, his parents, and his entire family.

I also conveyed to Chancellor Turner that there was a new urgency in the situation because L.D. and Jan's marriage was failing, and the couple was likely headed for a divorce. In view of such a possibility, L.D. was worried that his Faulkner collection would become a part of the divorce settlement and consequently might be sold off to the highest bidders. He wasn't concerned to deny Jan her share of the monetary value of the collection (Missouri is a communal property state), but he desperately wanted to ensure that the collection would remain intact.

There was one other factor that worked against Ole Miss's interests. It was a small matter, but sometimes small things impact big decisions. Ole Miss had received a federal grant to underwrite the travel of a number of Faulkner scholars to participate in a literary conference to be held in the Soviet Union. Joseph Blotner, Noel Polk, and a number of Ole Miss representatives, including Evans Harrington, the co-director of the annual Faulkner conference, were invited to make the trip. L.D. was extended an invitation as well, with the suggestion that he take along a few items from his collection to exhibit. But there was a condition: he would be expected to pay his own way. Offended at what he considered "second class" treatment, L.D. shared his anger with me.

I immediately called Evans Harrington.

"You folks can shoot yourselves in the foot more ways than I can count," I said. I went on to explain that L.D. knew that the other Faulkner scholars were not paying their own way.

Evans explained that L.D.'s invitation was an afterthought; he had not been included in the grant application. He added, "He's a millionaire. We figured he might like to go and could afford to pay for his own ticket."

"He's also the owner of a multi-million dollar Faulkner collection that Ole Miss wants," I countered.

After L.D. declined the invitation, Ole Miss invited Toby Holtzman, another Faulkner collector, to make the trip, and Holtzman accepted. I presume he bought his own airline ticket.

When L.D. asked me to arrange the meeting with Bill Stacy, he had been in discussions with Ole Miss for five and a half years, the last two of those with Chancellor Turner, but as yet no specific offer from the university had been forthcoming. And my discussions with Chancellor Turner had not altered the status quo.

There was one final episode in Ole Miss's pursuit of the collection. When it became apparent that they were losing the collection and it might be going to Southeast, Evans Harrington, the chairman of the English department, called me and offered me a position in the Ole Miss English department, with the clear implication that I should influence L.D. to send his collection to Ole Miss. I respectfully declined the offer. How could I be accepted and respected by my Ole Miss colleagues if they thought the only reason I got the job was because I had helped bring a Faulkner collection to Ole Miss?

The week after L.D.'s meeting with President Stacy, the president instructed our business office to issue a $1,000 check to L.D. as earnest money to secure ninety days for the university and L.D. to reach an agreement on the transfer of ownership of the Brodsky Collection to Southeast Missouri State University. Stacy also asked me to supply him with a position paper describing the uses the university could make of the collection. "I don't want the materials to sit behind glass in a museum," he said. "If they cannot be used by students and scholars, we don't want them."

I told my wife Kaye that L.D. would not cash the check. I felt that he was still hopeful and confident something could be worked out with Ole Miss and that the discussions with Southeast were at best a second alternative that, upon further reflection, he would abandon. It even entered my mind that L.D. had possibly entered into negotiations with Southeast to ratchet up the pressure on Ole Miss.

A few days later, however, Stacy informed me that L.D. had cashed the check and that lawyers and accountants representing both L.D. and Southeast were already engaged in negotiations. It was agreed that the first step in the process would be to obtain a professional appraisal of the collection by a neutral party.

Ralph Sipper and Larry Moskowitz, co-owners of Joseph the Provider Booksellers of Santa Barbara, California, two of the most highly respected rare book dealers in the country, were selected to conduct the appraisal. They traveled to Cape Girardeau in early July 1988, spending a week in the Rare Book Room and assigning a monetary value to every item in the Brodsky Collection, more than ten thousand items in all.

Sipper and Moskowitz delivered an appraisal of $3.1 million for the entire collection. Immediately, however, a problem surfaced. L.D. felt that several items, including the handwritten manuscript of Faulkner's short story "Wash" and the typescript of "Mississippi Poems," had been undervalued. When L.D. and the appraisers could not agree on a compromise figure for these items, the negotiations reached an impasse.

Stacy came up with a solution—but one that troubled me greatly. He would allow L.D. to retain the items he felt were under-appraised, and a deal would be struck for the remaining items. L.D. accepted that proposal, and I was heartbroken that several prize items had been excluded from the transaction.

Now came the big questions: what asking price would L.D. put on the collection, and could Southeast afford it? The figure L.D. settled on was $500,000, his estimate of the amount he had invested in the collection over the years. Interestingly, that figure was $250,000 less than his asking price of Ole Miss, despite the fact that the collection was now larger and thus appraised considerably higher than the figure he had used in the Ole Miss negotiations.

Since few except the largest universities, and certainly none like Southeast, have $500,000 available in ready cash to make a lump sum payment, L.D. offered a proposal. He would allow the university to pay him that amount, at a standard rate of interest, over twenty years. That method of payment would cost the university $50,000 a year for twenty years.

Provost Les Cochran was asked if he could find that amount in his annual budget for Academic Affairs. He said he could, explaining, "That's the cost of one teaching position per year, and we always have a few positions each year that go unfilled."

Thus the deal was finalized, well within the ninety days that Stacy and L.D. had agreed to. On July 25, 1988, Stacy invited L.D. and me to hand-deliver the Memorandum of Agreement to the home of Anne Bradshaw, president of the university's Board of Regents, for her signature. With her signature on the document, added to that of L.D., the Louis Daniel Brodsky Collection of William Faulkner Materials now belonged to Southeast Missouri State University.

Driving back to the campus to deliver the signed document to Stacy, I told L.D., using the words he had once used to me, "You've blown my cover." For ten years I had enjoyed a virtual monopoly on the scholarly use of the Brodsky Collection; now it was going to be opened to the world.

There still remained the troublesome question of those items that L.D. had held back from the original transaction. Neither L.D., Stacy, nor I was pleased that key items would not be coming to Southeast with the rest of the Brodsky Collection. So a solution to the problem had to be found.

Stacy and L.D. found that solution—and it was a very creative one. In those days, L.D. was paying commercial presses extremely high rates to design and print the poetry books for his Timeless Press (later Time Being Books). Stacy agreed to credit to L.D. $150,000 worth of printing services (at $15,000 per year for 10 years) in the University Print Shop in exchange for the remaining Faulkner documents in L.D.'s possession. It worked out as a perfect swap. The University got the rest of the Brodsky Collection, including some of its most prized items; in exchange, L.D. received not only better rates on his printing jobs but also the expert assistance of Gil Seres, the head of the printing office, and especially Ruth Dambach, a talented designer, in the production of the poetry books. In fact, Ruth proved to be an asset to L.D. even beyond his printing contract with the university.

When L.D. later hired his own designer and editor for Time Being Books, Ruth traveled to St. Louis to train that individual in the use of desktop-publishing software.

The contract for Southeast's acquisition of the Brodsky Collection was executed on September 1, 1988, and later that same month, L.D. and his father were jointly named the year's "Friend of the University." One of the highest honors associated with the university, this award is presented during Homecoming Week to individuals who have made outstanding contributions to the work and mission of the institution. That L.D. elected to have his father included in the recognition (and also to share the tax credit for the donated part of the collection) acknowledged not only the tremendous love and respect L.D. felt for his father but also the many contributions that Mr. Saul had made (in some cases unknowingly!) to the development of L.D.'s Faulkner collection.

My role in Southeast's acquisition of the Brodsky Collection has been much discussed by members of the Southeast community, both positively and negatively. Clearly, my decade-long collaboration with L.D. on his collection, especially the eight books we co-edited, along with the exhibits, lectures, and other activities we worked on together, provided a foundation of trust and achievement that the university could build on. However, as I noted previously, L.D.'s indication to Bill Stacy that he was considering placing the collection at Southeast was a complete surprise to me; and, in fact, as I have already indicated, I had been working hard behind the scenes to do everything I could to see that the collection went to Ole Miss.

Once I recognized that L.D. was serious about placing the collection at Southeast, of course I was elated, and from that point on I worked to help make that happen. However, it pains me to remember that in my hugest endeavor on behalf of Southeast, I failed miserably.

In the memorandum I sent to Bill Stacy on the prospect and feasibility of Southeast's owning and utilizing the Brodsky Collection, I indicated that there was an excellent possibility that the university could secure a Challenge Grant from the National Endowment for the Humanities to recover a good portion of the purchase price of the collection. In the mid-1980s, I had directed three Faulkner seminars in NEH's Summer Seminar for School Teachers program. In those three seminars I taught teachers from thirty-five different states and three overseas countries. A major reason I was selected to direct the seminars was my involvement with the Brodsky Collection, and in the course of that work I met and worked with several NEH executives, including Lynn Cheney, the NEH director, and Stephen Ross, a noted Faulkner scholar who was quite familiar with the Brodsky Collection and my Faulkner scholarship. Although the Challenge Grants department at NEH is separate from the Seminars division, I felt that my previous association with NEH and my familiarity with its programs, requirements, and application procedures would give Southeast an inside track on any request we made of the agency.

With the help of Southeast's Research and Grants office, I wrote a thirty-page application for a $500,000 NEH Challenge Grant to support our acquisition of the Brodsky Collection. Challenge Grants are 50/50 matching grants, with the applicant expected to supply half of the total funds. However, we anticipated that at least part of the gift portion of the Brodsky Collection could be applied toward the university's match of the NEH funds. Thus, if we could succeed in our application for the NEH grant, Southeast would acquire the Brodsky Collection at little to no expense.

Despite what our grants office and I considered an outstanding application, and despite the endorsements of U.S. Senators Christopher Bond and John Danforth and Representative Bill Emerson, we failed to get the grant. The evaluators noted the strength of the Brodsky Collection and the impressive and clearly stated plans for the university's use of it, but the matching fundraising plan needed to be strengthened, and (a bigger problem) some of the evaluators expressed skepticism about supporting a research collection at a non-research institution.

Not long afterward, even as we were still smarting from the rejection by NEH, there occurred a development that, had it occurred just a few months earlier, would in all likelihood have eliminated any chance for Southeast Missouri to acquire the Brodsky Collection: Governor John Ashcroft announced huge budget cuts to higher education, including a big part of the state funding to Southeast.

Immediately after the governor's announcement, Bill Stacy called me. He said, "When we acquired the Brodsky Collection, I needed the Challenge Grant. Now, I've got to have it."

All I could say in reply was, "I'll do my best."

The following year we rewrote our proposal to address the concerns of the evaluators and resubmitted the application, and this time the university's grants officer Adele Kupchella and I traveled to Washington to make our case personally to NEH. The Challenge Grants official received us very kindly, expressed admiration for our proposal, but then said, quite frankly, "If this application were coming from a Ph.D.-granting institution, it would fly through the approval process. But your school is not a research institution, and some evaluators might hold that against you."

At that I had to struggle mightily to maintain my self-control, but I managed to do so. I merely replied, "Well, there are many schools that would like to have this collection, and many people who think it should be somewhere else, but the fact is that Southeast Missouri State University owns the collection, and we feel we deserve the same support for it that any other school might receive. We pay taxes, too."

Several weeks later we heard for the second time that our application had been rejected—and for the reason that the officer had explained to us. I was devastated. And all these many years later, my disappointment has not abated. Failure to deliver on the Challenge Grant proposal, enabling Southeast to recover most of its investment in the Brodsky Collection, remains the largest disappointment, and the greatest failure, of my professional career.

The Center for Faulkner Studies

At its March 1989 meeting, the Southeast Missouri State University's Board of Regents voted to establish the Center for Faulkner Studies to utilize the recently acquired Brodsky Collection to sponsor and promote educational and research activities associated with Faulkner and related topics. At the same meeting I was appointed the first Director of the Center.

For its first eight years, the Center for Faulkner Studies existed largely in name only. Before the Brodsky Collection could be opened for public access, the materials had to be archived and cataloged, funds had to be found to finance the design and renovation of the Center's home in Kent Library, and operational procedures had to be established. During those years of preparation and waiting, the Center operated out of an unmarked storeroom on the fourth floor of the library and through its website.

The grand opening of the Center, originally located on the third floor of Kent Library, took place on March 4, 1997. The program featured remarks by L.D. Brodsky and tours of the Center and the Rare Book Room.

The year of the opening of the Faulkner Center happily coincided with the centennial of Faulkner's birth. As a result, Southeast and our Center for Faulkner Studies joined other institutions, organizations, and places in celebrating the one hundredth anniversary of Faulkner's birth. Our part of the centennial included a series of lectures and the unveiling of a Faulkner mural on the outer wall of the Faulkner Center in Kent Library. The lectures included addresses by Mississippi author Willie Morris, Faulkner scholar Charles Peek, L.D., and me. The mural, commissioned by Dean Martin Jones, was executed by Southeast art professor Grant Lund. I think that the painting—a brightly colored, abstract image of Faulkner superimposed on a reproduction of Faulkner's map of Yoknapatawpha County—is the best artistic depiction of Faulkner ever created.

The most impressive aspect of Grant's mural is the way the handling of perspective so perfectly mirrors the reading of a Faulkner novel. Standing immediately in front of the mural, the viewer sees only fragments and blotches of color, jigsaw puzzle pieces not yet arranged into a pattern—much like a first reading of the Benjy section in *The Sound and the Fury*. As one moves away from the mural, however, like reading the Benjy section a second or third time, the portrait of Faulkner gradually becomes clearer, sharper, finally assuming, from the end of the long hallway, an almost photographic quality. In Lund's painting, as in Faulkner's fiction, technique becomes theme.

As Grant painted his Faulkner mural on the wall, we invited various groups of students and townspeople to come to observe the work and interact with the artist. One day, when the mural was nearly finished, a group of Girl Scout Brownies came by to visit. I asked one of the young girls, "What do you think about the painting?" "It's awesome!" she responded. I asked, "Do you know whose picture that is?" She shook her head and said, "I don't know, but I think it's Abraham Lincoln."

In March 2016, the Faulkner Center moved into larger accommodations in room 406 of Kent Library. Upstairs from the Rare Book Room that houses the Brodsky Collection and adjacent to Special Collections, which partners with the Center in overseeing the Faulkner collection and hosting the research scholars who use it, the new location of the Center features larger offices, including one for visiting scholars, more exhibit space, an attractive conference room, and expanded storage areas. Organizationally, the Center functions as an auxiliary to the Department of English and the director answers to the chair of the English department and the dean of the College of Liberal Arts. This arrangement strikes some people as unusual, since at most institutions research materials like the Brodsky Faulkner collection would be under the sole management of Archives and Special Collections and used almost exclusively for research. However, since Southeast is a four-year, teaching institution with a master's program in many departments, and not a research institution granting doctoral degrees, we've sought ways to utilize the Brodsky Collection in the teaching function of the university, in addition to making it available to research scholars. For example, the Center sponsors lectures, conferences, public programs, and field trips that are aimed at contributing to the academic experiences of our students. The English department cooperates with the Center in offering Faulkner courses (sometimes teaming Faulkner with another author, such as "Faulkner and Twain," "Faulkner and Conrad," and "Faulkner and Morrison") and co-sponsoring summer seminars and other programs related to Faulkner and the Brodsky Collection. Professors bring their students to view the Faulkner materials in the Rare Book Room (it's no longer the room on campus that nobody ever enters), and students visit the Faulkner Center for advice and assistance on their term papers on Faulkner. Many other students from across the country and around the world request help through the Center's website. Each semester from one to three graduate students work as research assistants in the Center, and a number of those (and others of our students) choose to write master's theses on Faulkner. Bill Stacy's initial insistence that the Brodsky Collection be utilized in our curriculum and not become merely an exhibit of rarities under glass is being realized.

One area in which the Center chooses to specialize is the international study of Faulkner. Since its inception the Faulkner Center has hosted scholars from Canada, England, France, Germany, Croatia, Romania, the Republic of Georgia, Japan, China, Taiwan, South Korea, Nigeria, and the United Arab Emirates. Some come to conduct research in the Brodsky Collection for their doctoral dissertations, books, and scholarly articles. Some come to attend the biannual conferences. Some come simply to view signed books and handwritten manuscripts by and photographs of the world-famous author.

The largest number of international visitors to the Center come from Japan and China. Since 1999, BioKyowa, Inc.—a Japanese-American business located in Cape Girardeau, with headquarters in Tokyo—has provided an annual travel award that enables a visiting Japanese scholar to spend up to two weeks at the Faulkner Center, utilizing the Brodsky Collection for research, delivering a public lecture, and participating in other types of cultural exchange. The BioKyowa award honors the special relationship that Faulkner developed with Japan during his visit to that country in 1955.

Each year since 2006, one to four Chinese professors have spent from six months to a full year studying at the Center, and that number is steadily increasing. The highest total occurred in 2013, when there were five Chinese scholars in residence at the Center; they came from universities in Xi'an, Qingdao, and Jinan. Dr. Christopher Rieger, my successor as Director of the Faulkner Center, and I (now a Professor Emeritus) hold weekly tutorials with all of the visiting scholars, discussing with them Faulkner's texts, the most useful of the critical studies devoted to his work (most of which are not available to them in China), and their own research projects.

The first Chinese scholar to visit the Faulkner Center was Changlei Li, at that time a literature professor at Weifang City University in Shandong Province and now dean of the School of Foreign Languages at the University of Jinan and one of the foremost Faulkner scholars in all of China. Changlei spent a year in Cape Girardeau, and Kaye and I practically adopted him as a member of our family. During his year with us, he conducted research for his doctoral dissertation on Faulkner, a Lacanian analysis of various Faulkner characters. As I read the progressive drafts of his study, I advised him to include the works of some Chinese Faulkner scholars in his research, since his dissertation was being completed for a Chinese university.

Shortly after his return to China, Changlei arranged for Kaye and me to visit China and for me to give a series of lectures at three universities. In Jinan we were treated to a banquet, and the director of Changlei's dissertation, Professor Guo, was one of our hosts. In the course of the evening, I mentioned to him how impressed I was with Changlei's progress on his dissertation, to which Professor Guo replied, "Yes, but, you know, there are some Chinese scholars who know something about Faulkner." I didn't tell him of my previous advice to Changlei.

During the last three days of our stay in China, Changlei had to excuse himself as our host, arranging for one of his friends to take over as our guide. Changlei explained that the deadline for the completion of his dissertation was the following week, and Professor Guo was requiring him to rewrite certain sections to incorporate Chinese scholarship in his study. Given Changlei's anxiety regarding the situation, I refrained from saying, "I told you so."

On that same trip to China, Kaye and I were honored with a luncheon in Weifang City, hosted by the university president, who is also Party Secretary of the Communist Party. A Chinese banquet includes several toasts to the honored guests. But since I was scheduled to give a lecture immediately following the meal, I was trying to avoid drinking a lot of wine, taking only a small sip with each toast. The Party Secretary would have none of that. At the next toast, he lifted his glass to me, said, "Dr. Hamblin, chug-a-lug" (the Chinese variation of "Bottoms up"), and drained his entire glass. I, of course, had no choice (to Changlei's great amusement, I might add) but to follow suit. I'm always very nervous before I speak in public, but that day I found myself extremely relaxed and confident.

I've benefitted greatly, both professionally and personally, from my interactions with the international scholars. English-speaking readers of Faulkner tend to view him as a "Southern" writer, and they typically read his novels and stories as a gloss on the history of the American South—from the displacement of Native Americans by white settlers, through the years of chattel slavery and the plantation system, on through the Civil War, Reconstruction, and Jim Crow, to the early years of the civil rights movement. Many international readers of Faulkner, however, know little if anything of this Southern history; they enjoy reading Faulkner for his character types, themes, and narrative techniques. Thus we instruct one another. Chris Rieger and I take the international scholars to Oxford to immerse them in Faulkner's native locale; they teach us how to read Faulkner from a "global" perspective. And in the course of these exchanges, I acquire many new friends from different parts of the globe.

L.D. also enjoyed interacting with our international visitors, frequently driving down from St. Louis to host the visiting scholars in the Rare Book Room, recounting for them stories associated with the Faulkner artifacts in his collection. He also occasionally invited the scholars to join him for outings in St. Louis. One of his favorite scholars was Masako Umegaki of Nagoya (Japan) University of Foreign Studies, who spent nine months at the Faulkner Center in 2009. At L.D.'s invitation, Kaye and I drove Masako to St. Louis, and the three of us spent the day with L.D., visiting the art museum and the Missouri Botanical Gardens. Perhaps L.D.'s favorite place in all of St. Louis was the Japanese garden that is a part of the Botanical site. That day he greatly enjoyed strolling through the garden with an individual who understands and appreciates the patterns and symbolism of Japanese landscape art.

Masako was also introduced that day to L.D.'s sense of humor. As we drove past the St. Louis Zoo on our way to the Botanical Gardens, Masako asked, "What would be the featured animals in this zoo?" L.D. replied, "Just the ordinary types, like unicorns and dragons."

Another specialized focus of the Faulkner Center is the classroom teaching of Faulkner's works. An outgrowth of my involvement with the "Teaching Faulkner" sessions at the Faulkner and Yoknapatawpha Conference, this aspect of the Center's activities encourages a network of high school, college, and university teachers of Faulkner. The "Teaching Faulkner" site on the Center's website publishes articles that have particular relevance for classroom teachers. Initially, we also published a "Teaching Faulkner" newsletter that was mailed to more than two hundred teachers; now the newsletter is produced in an electronic edition for the internet. All such activities are designed to assist teachers with their questions about which of Faulkner's novels and stories work best in the classroom, which teaching strategies to use, and how to deal with Faulkner's characters' use of the word "nigger."

Since 2006, the Faulkner Center has hosted a bi-annual conference focusing on the intertextual reading of Faulkner and one other writer Our first conference focused on Faulkner and Twain, and succeeding conferences have dealt with Faulkner and Kate Chopin, Faulkner and Toni Morrison, Faulkner and Robert Penn Warren, Faulkner and Zora Neale Hurston, and Faulkner and Ernest Hemingway. Each of these conferences has attracted presenters from fifteen to twenty American states and several foreign countries. A book of selected essays from each conference is published for the Center for Faulkner Studies by Southeast Missouri State University Press.

Although there is considerable daily activity going on in the Faulkner Center, the heart and soul of the Faulkner Center operation is the Center's website, together with the Facebook page that Dr. Rieger has added to the Center's internet presence. We conduct a huge "mail-order business" from Room 406 of Kent Library, sending scholars electronic scans of documents from the Brodsky Collection, answering questions for researchers, recommending sources for students, and serving as fact-checkers for such organizations as academic publishers, the *New York Times*, and television shows like *Jeopardy*.

We even have a fun feature on the Center's webpage. Faulkner has become something of an icon in popular culture, and we ask our website's users to post Faulkner "sightings" they have witnessed. Yes, Faulkner is more apt to be "cited" than "sighted"; but, like Elvis, he continues to show up quite frequently—in movies and television shows, in news broadcasts, in books by other authors, in the lyrics of popular songs, even in advertisements for everything from whiskey to ink pens.

The latest of the activities of the Faulkner Center has been the development of two Faulkner MOOCs (Massive Online Open Classes) taught by Dr. Rieger and me. The first, "Faulkner 101," which has enrolled participants from two dozen different countries, examines *As I Lay Dying*, *The Sound and the Fury*, and *Light in August*. The second, "Faulkner and Southern History," examines *The Unvanquished*, *Absalom, Absalom!*, and *Go Down, Moses*.

SOME PROBLEMS SURFACE

Southeast Missouri State University's Center for Faulkner Studies is now internationally recognized as one of the major contributors to the field of Faulkner Studies. Such success, however, did not come easily, as the early years of the Center's operation were marked by controversy and misunderstanding. One decision relating to the acquisition of the Brodsky Collection and the establishment of the Faulkner Center proved to be especially controversial and troublesome. As part of his negotiations with Brodsky, Stacy appointed L.D. to a twenty-year term as faculty curator of the collection at a part-time salary of $40,000 per year. When this arrangement was made public, there was vehement objection from many on the Southeast faculty. The Faculty Senate took up the issue, an underground campus newsletter mocked President Stacy and Provost Cochran, and an editorial in the local newspaper, the *Southeast Missourian*, questioned the university's decision making. The fact that the university faculty had not received a raise the previous year added fuel to the fire of their anger. Also an expressed issue of concern was that the acquisition of the Brodsky Collection was a top-down decision with little input from deans, chairs, and faculty.

Cochran sought to explain to the Faculty Senate that the capital funds used to acquire the Brodsky Collection could not legally have been spent on faculty salaries, but his arguments went unheeded. Even his statement that the money very likely "would have gone to athletics instead" was ignored.

I tried as best I could to keep a low profile during the debate—and to shield L.D. from the negative publicity. When the Faculty Senate "subpoenaed" me to come and explain things to the senators, I refused to go. The deal was done; there would be no undoing of it. Besides, I was pleased that the humanities and the library had benefitted from a budget decision for a change.

What few people realized in all the heated furor—and many do not understand even today—was that Bill Stacy had a larger goal in mind than just acquiring the Brodsky Collection. During the negotiations with the Brodsky family, Bill developed a high regard and great respect not only for L.D. but also for his father, Saul; and both L.D. and Mr. Saul developed a great affection for Bill. Stacy was convinced that the Brodskys would be a future asset not only to the university but to the larger community of Cape Girardeau as well.

The son of a poor Russian immigrant, Saul Brodsky owned and operated Biltwell Company, a clothing manufacturing business, for almost fifty years, specializing in moderately priced, private-label dress slacks, suits, and sports coats. As president, and later as board chairman, Mr. Brodsky developed Biltwell into one of the top men's clothing manufacturers in the nation, best known for its John Alexander brand.

L.D. fondly recalled the times when, as a young boy, he traveled with his father by train to New York, where Mr. Brodsky would rent a hotel room, spread his samples around the room, and welcome wholesalers and retailers who visited the room to place orders. L.D. also remembered the time that Ben Hogan, the famous golfer, visited the Brodskys' home in St. Louis to finalize an endorsement contract with Biltwell.

Mr. Brodsky invested much of the profit from his manufacturing business into real estate projects in St. Louis. As a developer and investor, Mr. Brodsky was co-owner of the Breckenridge St. Louis Frontenac Hotel (now the Hilton St. Louis Frontenac Hotel) and Le Chateau Village in Frontenac, and was a principal partner in the development of Northwest Plaza.

This was a man any university or community would be thrilled to be associated with.

In 1988, the downtown area of Cape Girardeau was literally falling into the river. Businesses were abandoning downtown for the west of town, along the interstate, and homeowners were heading for the suburbs. Empty storefronts, littered streets, decaying houses, and increasing crime defined the downtown area. Even the river itself was being abandoned, portions of its historic, bricked waterfront allowed to crumble to pieces and be swept away by the frequent spring floods. Visitors to the riverfront, like Faulkner scholar Jim Carothers of the University of Kansas, were claiming the bricks as souvenirs.

Bill Stacy had weekly reminders of this situation. As president of Southeast, he held a seat on the Cape Girardeau Chamber of Commerce, for a number of terms serving as president of the Chamber. He and Mayor Howard Tooke had shepherded the negotiations that resulted in the joint university-city partnership to build the Show Me Center, a sports arena and performance center, but ambitious plans to restore and use the old Marquette Hotel and the historic St. Vincent Seminary had come to naught.

Two businessmen who were heavily invested in the downtown area were Martin Hecht and Sidney Pollack, both of whom had served on the university's Board of Regents and were good friends and supporters of Bill Stacy. Bill introduced the Brodskys to Hecht and Pollack, who, along with Stacy, encouraged Mr. Saul to consider investing in downtown Cape. Not long afterward, Roger Brodsky, L.D.'s brother, moved to Cape Girardeau and opened a business, Pet World, on Main Street. Roger's larger purpose was to get to know the community, meet the business leaders, assess the opportunity for investment in the downtown area, and report back to Mr. Saul. Stacy's hiring of L.D. to work part-time on behalf of the university was also a part of this larger plan.

Unfortunately, nothing came of this grand design. In 1989, Stacy resigned as president of Southeast to become the first president of a newly established institution, California State University at San Marcos. Not long after that, both Hecht and Pollack moved from Cape Girardeau, and Roger Brodsky returned to St. Louis. Downtown Cape would continue its decline until the completion of the university's River Campus in 2007 and the opening of the Isle Casino in 2012 put Old Town Cape back on an upward curve.

Even though the hope of involving the Brodskys in a much larger role in the university and community was never realized, it can still be argued that hiring Brodsky as curator of his collection was a good investment for the university. In that capacity, L.D. continued his Faulkner collecting, but now for the university rather than for himself. However, since the university or Kent Library had little funding available for acquisitions, a creative way had to be found to finance L.D.'s efforts. To address this issue, the University Foundation, under the direction of Robert W. Foster, established a line of credit for L.D. that allowed him to acquire materials that came available and then to repay the loan by selling some of the duplicate items in the collection. All such transactions, of course, had to be jointly approved by the university and L.D.

L.D. and I had discussed much earlier the greater importance of letters, manuscripts, and documents for researchers than signed copies of first editions. A signed book will tell a scholar where the author was on the date he signed the book (and, in Faulkner's case, whether he was drunk or sober)—and little else. By contrast, letters, manuscripts, wills, and photographs are far more valuable aids for scholars researching an author's life and works. The Blotner Papers are a prime case in point. While it was always painful to surrender a precious book personally inscribed by Faulkner, L.D. recognized the occasional need to do so in the interest of the greater research value of the collection.

Over the course of his tenure as curator of the university's Faulkner collection, almost $2 million of additional items were added. Some of these were paid for by swapping or selling books from the collection, but other items were paid for and donated by L.D. His last gifts to the collection, made in 2013, were Faulkner's "Pocket Ben" watch, signed by Faulkner on the back, and the Royal typewriter on which Faulkner typed some of his later work, including large portions of his novel *A Fable*. These two items alone were professionally appraised at $450,000. Just recently, a noted New York book dealer, one who is quite familiar with the Faulkner market and the Brodsky Collection, conservatively estimated the value of the Brodsky Collection in today's dollars to be $15–20 million.

Thus, under L.D.'s curatorship, the Brodsky Collection not only appreciated in monetary value but, more importantly for its intended purpose, was transformed into a far more useful study and research collection—one that Joel Williamson, the noted historian from the University of North Carolina at Chapel Hill, called "one of the finest research collections in the United States." Williamson used the Brodsky Collection for two consecutive summers and found it to be an invaluable aid in producing his book, *William Faulkner and Southern History*.

I believe at this point in history—nearly thirty years later—any reasonably minded individual would conclude that the University got its money's worth in its dealings with L.D. Brodsky.

Not all of the criticism of the university's acquisition of the Brodsky Collection was directed at Stacy, L.D., and Cochran. Understandably, I received my share of it as well. And it continued for a number of years.

After the university had acquired the Brodsky Collection and discussions were underway about the creation of the Center for Faulkner Studies, Provost Cochran called me to his office. It had already been agreed that I would become the Center director and would receive, as is typical for faculty assuming part-time administrative appointments, some release time from my teaching duties. But I asked for more.

"Let's see, the University gets a three-million-dollar collection, Brodsky gets one million dollars, and I get three hours of release time," I told the provost. I added, "Everybody knows that release time is the way universities get work done they don't want to pay for."

"So, what do you want?" Cochran asked.

"I want one of those distinguished professorships you've promised to the faculty," I replied.

The year before, in his campaign to sell our faculty on the idea for market pay to professors in the sciences, business, and technology, Cochran had proposed to create a dozen distinguished professorships in the humanities as a means of balancing the score. A news article quoting him on that intent had appeared on the front page of the *Southeast Missourian*. So I asked for one of those positions.

"I can't do that," Cochran said. "We're not going to be able to create the distinguished professorships." (The university did go ahead and adopt market pay, however.)

Then he added: "But I can give you the money."

Most academics I know care more about money than about titles, and that's certainly true in my case. So I told Cochran, "Thanks, I accept the offer."

Thus I became the founding director of the Center for Faulkner Studies, with a one-course reduction in my teaching schedule each semester, guaranteed summer employment, and a modest stipend (roughly equivalent to that paid at the time to department heads) added to my regular salary.

University administrations typically change quite frequently (I worked for eight presidents during my fifty years at Southeast), and I've noticed that new administrators are sometimes reluctant to honor the agreements established by their predecessors. I soon found this to be the case when Kala Stroup and Charles Kupchella became, respectively, the new president and new provost at Southeast.

Soon after her arrival on campus in 1990, Dr. Stroup told me that one of the things that had most impressed her about Southeast was the Brodsky Collection and its potential for development and usage. However, after the Faculty Senate raised its voice protesting the university's deal with Brodsky—and after the *Southeast Missourian* published its scathing (and factually erroneous) editorial criticizing both the university and Brodsky—Dr. Stroup called me to her office and, concerning the plans for the Brodsky Collection and Faulkner Center, pronounced, "We're going to have to lie low for a while, but then we'll come back strong."

Then, worse news, "We'll need to delay the reception for the Brodskys."

A couple of weeks previously, Dr. Stroup had told me she wanted to host a reception for the Brodsky family at Wildwood, the university's presidential home. With L.D.'s help, I began putting together a mailing list for invitations. Now, the reception was off, and I'd have to come up with some excuse for the Brodskys as to why.

Perhaps unwisely, I left that meeting with a word of advice to the president. "You need to learn who your friends are. You'll never please your critics, and if you try to please them, you'll wind up alienating your friends. And then everybody will be against you."

With Bill Stacy's resignation in 1989, Bob Foster's retirement in 1991, and Les Cochran's departure in 1992 to become president of Youngstown State University, the three Southeast administrators who were most instrumental in the acquisition of the Brodsky Collection, the creation of the Faulkner Center, and the support of both by the University Foundation were now gone. The Faulkner Center still had the support of my chairperson, Robert Burns (and, after him, Carol Scates), and the dean of the College of Liberal Arts, Martin Jones; but no one at the higher levels of administration seemed much committed to the Center—and some seemed in distinct opposition to it.

One day Dean Jones, who was in a position to recognize before I did the degree of the opposition to Brodsky and me, from both faculty and administrators, called me to ask if I had a written contract reflecting the agreement I had with Cochran. I said no, it was just a mutual understanding, although my pay stubs would evidence what that understanding was. He said I needed a written contract, and he offered to draft one for me, reflecting the policy that was then in place. As events transpired, Dean Jones's action was a godsend.

With Cochran's departure, Charles Kupchella, who had previously worked with Stroup at Murray State University, became provost. Almost immediately, and I assume with President Stroup's approval, he set about seeking to restructure the contracts that both L.D. and I had with the university. L.D.'s contract was too loosely defined; his job description needed to include more specified duties, perhaps even regular office hours. If such was not agreeable to L.D., then his designated relationship with the university would have to be changed from "faculty" to "contractor." In my case, the released time for summer would have to be restructured and the stipend would need to be discontinued, since (or so I was told) other center directors on campus did not receive stipends. Coincidentally, I knew this last claim to be untrue, at least in one instance, since I played basketball twice a week with another center director who received a stipend—one considerably larger than mine.

L.D. was offended to be asked to give up his "faculty" status (as well as his parking permit), but since his annual salary was not affected, he reluctantly accepted his new designation. I refused, however, to accept the elimination of my stipend and would not sign the revised contract that Kupchella presented to me. This impasse lasted for almost a year, at the end of which I was determined to resign as director of the Faulkner Center, return to full-time teaching in the English department, and start planning for my retirement at age sixty-five.

Dale Nitzschke, the next president of Southeast, saved the day— and in so doing extended my professional career by several years. Stroup resigned her position in 1995 (with the Faulkner Center still "lying low" and the Brodsky family reception still "postponed") to become the Commissioner of Higher Education for the State of Missouri. Nitzschke assumed the presidency in July 1996, and in the fall of that year made a round of visits to every department on campus. When he came to the English department, he asked our faculty to introduce ourselves and indicate how many years we had taught at Southeast.

When my turn came, I stated my name and said I had been teaching at the school for thirty-one years.

He said, "That's a long time to teach in one place. This must be a pretty good school."

I replied, "It used to be."

At the conclusion of the meeting Nitzschke lingered in the hallway and called me aside as I exited the room. He said, "I was struck by what you said in there. Come by my office sometime and let's talk about it."

When we met I presented an overview of the history of the Faulkner Center and described the complications that had developed with the Faculty Senate, Stroup, and Kupchella. Nitzschke listened politely and then asked, "What do you expect from a college administrator?"

I replied, "I expect the same thing that an administrator would expect from a faculty member—that one honor and fulfill any contract that has been agreed to."

In a couple of days, Kupchella called to say he wished to meet with me—and not in his office. I said he was welcome to come to the Faulkner Center. Before I left for work the next day I told Kaye, "I don't think I'll have to worry about writing that letter of resignation. I'm going to be fired."

At the meeting, however, Kupchella informed me that President Nitzschke had instructed him to continue my existing contract, which I now had in writing, thanks to Dean Jones. In further discussions, I agreed to restructure my summer assignment, as Kupchella requested, but my appointment as director and the stipend would remain in effect.

Kupchella became president of the University of North Dakota in 1999, and Jane Stephens replaced him as the Southeast provost. During her tenure, the Center for Faulkner Studies experienced tremendous growth and success, establishing itself as a major player in the field of Faulkner studies, both in the U.S. and abroad. Stephens deserves a great deal of credit for that success.

Stephens had been successively a history professor, director of the Honors Program, and assistant provost at Southeast from 1978 to 1994, before leaving to become executive vice-chancellor of the University of South Carolina at Spartanburg. She was assistant provost to Les Cochran when Southeast acquired the Brodsky Collection, thus she was privy to all the ups and downs that characterized the early history of the Faulkner Center. Her return to Southeast as provost was viewed favorably by our entire faculty, but by no one more than me.

Stephens pledged her full support to the development and expansion of the Faulkner Center. In return for that support, she made three demands: one, that the inventory and cataloging of the Brodsky Collection be completed posthaste; two, that the Center's website be improved and expanded; and three, that the Center host periodic conferences focusing on Faulkner and related topics.

The conference issue had been a lingering problem. Stephens knew that Cochran and I had originally agreed that the Center would host conferences, but amid all the ensuing controversy, that plan had been derailed. I realize in retrospect that allowing that to happen was a mistake. But criticism and negativity erode confidence, and lacking confidence, one is reluctant to take risks. The simple fact is that I was afraid to organize a conference in those early years because I could not guarantee its success; and its failure, I felt certain, would be highlighted by opponents as another argument against the Brodsky Collection, the Faulkner Center, and me. As all athletes, performers, and entrepreneurs know, the first step to success is overcoming the fear of failure. But that first step may be the most difficult one of all. And it is made all the more difficult when you know that there are others who are eager to see you fail.

In any event, Stephens would not allow me to procrastinate any longer, so we began organizing our first conference, which we hosted in 2006. Titled "Faulkner and Twain," it attracted presenters from fifteen different states and four foreign countries. In addition to the formal papers and panels by professors and graduate students, the program included a keynote address by Southern literature expert Robert Brinkmeyer, then of the University of Arkansas but now of the University of South Carolina; a visit to the Rare Book Room to view the Brodsky Collection and chat with L.D.; and a readers' theater presentation written and directed by Southeast instructor Roseanna Whitlow and featuring two local actors, Patrick Abbott and Lester Goodin, portraying Faulkner and Twain. Our Southeast Missouri State University Press subsequently published the conference proceedings in a book, *Faulkner and Twain*, coedited by Melanie Speight, a research assistant in the Center, and me—and contracted with the Faulkner Center for an ongoing series of books based on our forthcoming conferences. Conferees even expressed their joy in attending a conference in a small city instead of the usual metropolitan setting. Given the many positive results of this first conference, it appears that I need not have worried about failure at all.

The success of that first conference (and the five that have followed it) validated the dream that L.D. and I had at the very beginning: that the Brodsky Collection and the Center for Faulkner Studies would encourage students and scholars in the study of Faulkner and over the years draw many of them to the campus of Southeast Missouri State University. While we had had to wait a little longer than we anticipated for the dream to begin to materialize, it was proving to be well worth the wait.

Further Acquisitions

From the very beginning it was the hope of all of us—L.D., Jim Zink, me, and the university—that the acquisition of the Brodsky Collection and the creation of the Faulkner Center might serve as a catalyst to enable our archives to grow and expand. And such proved to be the case, sometimes in very interesting and unpredictable ways.

In 2006, I was granted a sabbatical leave to complete a research project. My chairperson, Carol Scates, asked me if I knew someone who could fill in for me while I was away. I told her I knew just the person, if he were willing to do it.

William Frank, emeritus professor of English and a former dean at Longwood University in Farmville, Virginia, had been one of my favorite professors at Delta State University and a colleague during my first five years at Southeast. Bill and his wife, Angie, eagerly accepted our invitation, glad for the opportunity to return to a campus and community they liked and to renew acquaintance with longtime friends.

During his visiting professorship, Bill invited Michael Lund, one of his friends and colleagues at Longwood, to come to Southeast to present a reading from his latest novel. Lund, a native of Rolla, Missouri, is the author of a popular series of novels set alongside the historic American highway, Route 66. Michael seized the opportunity afforded by his return to Missouri to invite his brother Carl, a physicist who lives in New Mexico, to meet him in Cape Girardeau, since the town is located roughly equidistant from their respective homes in the East and the West.

During the Lunds' visit to our campus, Bill asked me to show them the Faulkner collection in our Rare Book Room. There, one afternoon, I showed Michael and Carl handwritten letters, manuscripts, inscribed books, and (to the especial delight of Carl the physicist) the presentation copy of Albert Einstein's *Ideas and Opinions* that Einstein personally inscribed to Faulkner.

The Lunds' visit to the Southeast campus was a great success. Michael's presentation was well received by the students and guests in attendance, the two brothers had a good reunion with one another, and Kaye and I (and others) had acquired two new friends.

Not long after Michael had returned to Virginia, he sent me an email message, inquiring whether Faulkner and William Carlos Williams had any connection with one another. I jokingly replied that they had once been in the same room together, the two of them serving in 1956 on the Writers' Committee in President Eisenhower's People-to-People program. (Transcripts of some of those committee meetings are included in the Brodsky Collection.) I pointed out that, while the two authors were undoubtedly aware of each other's work and reputation, I doubted if there was ever very much personal interaction between them.

I was greatly surprised when Michael wrote back to explain that the reason he was asking about any connection between the two authors was that he and his brother Carl possessed the original typescript of a poem that Williams had written about their mother when she was a little girl and given to that little girl's mother, the Lund brothers' grandmother. A physician, Williams had diagnosed (falsely, as it turned out) the ten-year-old girl as having leukemia, and he wrote a poem about the beautiful girl and gave it to her mother, a neighbor and fellow poet. The poem, "about a little girl," had remained in the Macy/Lund family for eighty-five years and had never been published. Now that both the recipient and the subject of the poem were deceased, Michael and Carl were trying to decide what to do with the manuscript. Given their sentimental connection to the poem's subject and origin, they were not interested in selling it. As Missouri natives, they had wondered about placing the poem at some Missouri institution, and since they had been impressed with Southeast's care and use of its Faulkner collection, they were now thinking that the Southeast archives might be an appropriate place for the manuscript to find its permanent home.

Once the Lunds made their decision to place their beloved manuscript at Southeast, Bill Frank, Special Collections librarian Dr. Lisa Speer, and I began planning a coming-out party for the little girl of the poem. We settled on a public program in March 2007, which would feature Michael's story of the origin and history of the poem, my critical commentary on the text, and Michael's formal presentation of the manuscript to the university. On the day of the program, an

Associated Press wire story carried worldwide the news of the emergence of the poem and its donation to Southeast Missouri State University. The next year, Michael and I co-authored a book on the amazing history of the poem.

In 1998, Jane Isbell Haynes, an independent Faulkner scholar and collector from Memphis who had moved to Irvine, California, donated her cache of Faulkner materials to the Center for Faulkner Studies. Jane was a remarkable individual. A church archivist, businesswoman, manager of her family farm, and mother of three children, Haynes did not become interested in Faulkner until age sixty, when she attended a Faulkner seminar at Southwestern (now Rhodes College) in Memphis. Following that seminar, she began visiting antiquarian book stores to acquire Faulkner books to read.

Haynes went on to become an avid Faulkner collector and author of numerous treatments of the author's life and works, including two books dealing with Faulkner's ancestry and background: *William Faulkner: His Tippah County Heritage* and *William Faulkner: His Lafayette County Heritage*. She continued reading and writing about Faulkner into her nineties. Her recent essay in the *Mississippi Quarterly*—published shortly before her death—undoubtedly gives her the distinction of being the oldest Faulkner scholar to publish an article on the famous author.

Over the years, L.D. Brodsky provided helpful advice and assistance to Jane, and it was principally her gratitude to L.D. that led her to place her Faulkner materials with his at Southeast. "I have long admired the work that Mr. Brodsky and Dr. Hamblin are doing," Jane said at the time of her donation, "and I'm very pleased that my Faulkner collection will be preserved and made available for scholars and students to use." Along with other items, those materials include the research files for her two Faulkner books and rare historic photographs of the Mississippi towns of Ripley and Oxford, both closely associated with Faulkner.

But there was one item that Jane did not part with in her original donation to the Faulkner Center. That was a handwritten manuscript by Faulkner entitled "Sorority."

Jane recounts the history of this manuscript in a monograph published by Seajay Press in 1983. The one-page manuscript was penned by Faulkner in 1933 as a gift to a young female college student, the roommate of Faulkner's stepdaughter, Victoria, at Mississippi Synodical College in Holly Springs, Mississippi. During a visit with Victoria at Rowan Oak, the student asked Faulkner if he would make a copy for her of the pledge used by her sorority. Faulkner gladly obliged, taking the copy of the pledge the student provided and disappearing into his study. A short while later he returned and handed the student a statement written in his small, meticulous handwriting. Only after she was back home did the student examine the manuscript carefully and realize that Faulkner had not copied the pledge she had given him, but instead had substituted his own original idea of the purpose and ideals of a sororal organization. Years later Jane acquired the document from the original owner.

In 2007, I wrote to Jane, asking if she still possessed the "Sorority" document and, if so, what she planned to do with it. I suggested, naturally, that the logical place for its eventual deposit was with her other Faulkner materials in our Center for Faulkner Studies.

Jane wrote back to inform me that the manuscript, for safekeeping, was in the possession of her son, Dr. Barton Haynes, director of Duke University's Human Vaccine and Immunology Institute and head of a world research consortium (CHAVI) seeking a vaccine and cure for AIDS. Jane said she would talk with Barton to get his thoughts regarding the disposition of the document.

A few days later, I received an email message from Dr. Haynes, indicating that the Faulkner document belonged to his mother and that the decision was totally hers on what to do with it. Dr. Haynes noted that he was an admirer of Faulkner's writing, but he greatly preferred Willa Cather and his collecting interests had been directed to Cather rather than Faulkner.

In our exchange of messages I mentioned to Barton that, coincidentally, a good friend of mine also works on the medical staff at Duke. Dr. Mark Stacy, the son of Bill Stacy, the Southeast president who negotiated the acquisition of the Brodsky Collection, is Professor of Neurology and Vice Dean for Clinical Research in Duke's medical school. One of the world's leading authorities on Parkinson's disease, Mark as a youngster had played on a church basketball team that I coached. Barton wrote back that his family and Mark's family were the closest of friends. Great, I thought, maybe Mark will give me a good character reference.

Shortly thereafter, Jane notified me that she had decided to donate the "Sorority" manuscript to our Faulkner Center. Of course I was elated and wanted to secure the manuscript as quickly as possible. My first thought was that perhaps Mark Stacy could deliver the manuscript to me the next time he visited his family in Cape Girardeau, but Mark informed me that it might be some time before he would make that trip. So I told Jane that I would drive to Durham to retrieve the manuscript.

Thus, in July 2007, Kaye and I made the trip to Durham. We invited Jane Stacy, Mark's mother, to accompany us. In Durham, while Jane visited with her son and grandchildren, Kaye and I met Barton Haynes and his family, learned of his AIDS research in Africa, Thailand, and elsewhere, discussed literature and his mother's interest in Faulkner—and left with "Sorority" in our possession. On the return trip to Cape Girardeau, I was so nervous with the manuscript in my possession that I refused to leave the document in the car when we stopped at restaurants or rest areas. Upon arrival back home, I went straight to the Rare Book Room and placed "Sorority" with our other Faulkner treasures.

In 1997, Michele Crouther, a high school English teacher from Ste. Genevieve, Missouri, was enrolled in one of my graduate seminars. During our discussion of Faulkner I mentioned his ancestral connection to her hometown. Michelle already knew this and informed me that one of her neighbors, Mrs. Anna Thomure, who claimed kinship with Faulkner, had told her that she possessed a family letter that proved the relationship. I asked Michele to see if she could arrange for me to view the letter, and at the next class meeting she brought me a photocopy of the letter that Mrs. Thomure had supplied. As soon as I read it, I knew I was looking at indisputable proof that Faulkner's ancestor did indeed migrate to Mississippi from Ste. Genevieve, Missouri.

The letter, dated July 19, 1863, is written and signed by J.W. Falkner, the brother of William C. Falkner, William Faulkner's great-grandfather. The letter is posted from a prisoner of war camp on Johnson's Island, near Sandusky, Ohio, where the author, a Confederate captain, is imprisoned following his capture near Holly Springs, Mississippi. The salutation is to "Sis," almost certainly a sister-in-law, the widow of his deceased brother, Anderson, and the body of the letter supplies information on the Mississippi Falkners to relatives back in Ste. Genevieve. For example, the mother [Caroline] is said to be in Ripley, and "Brother Bill" [William C. Falkner] is identified as a brigadier general in the Confederate army (in actuality he was a colonel). J.W. notes that it has been two years since he has had any news from the Missouri relatives (he specifically names sisters Caroline and Jettie, as well as Thomas, probably a nephew), and he describes the negative effects of the war on his finances. He adds that he expects to be freed in an exchange of prisoners fairly soon (as he was).

Of course, I dearly wanted to add the letter to our Faulkner collection, but the owner was not willing to part with it. So I had to be contented with the photocopy.

Flash forward to 2013, when the staff of the Southeast Archives was in the process of developing a digitalization project in conjunction with the 150th anniversary of the Civil War. A public call went out for letters and other documents relating to the war, and Mrs. Patricia Parker, heir to Mrs. Thomure and now the possessor of the J.W. Falkner letter, offered it to be scanned into the project's website. Interestingly, the archivist who arranged for the use of the letter had no idea initially that the letter had any connection to William Faulkner; it was merely a Civil War document like the others being included in the project. Because of that association, the letter was borrowed, scanned, and posted on the website "Confluence and Crossroads: The Civil War in the American Heartland"—all without my knowledge.

Mrs. Parker, of course, knew of the rumored connection of the letter to William Faulkner, and (another fortunate coincidence) shortly after lending the letter to the Southeast archives, she read in the St. Louis paper an article about our Faulkner collection and decided that our collection would be an appropriate place for the letter to be permanently housed.

My involvement in these developments came back into play when I received a call from a former student, Bryan Hollenbach, a reporter for the *Ste. Genevieve Herald*, wanting to interview me about the Falkner letter that two Southeast archivists—Roxanne Dunn and A.J. Medlock—were coming to Ste. Genevieve to obtain from Mrs. Parker. I told Bryan this was all news to me, but I would check with Ms. Dunn and get back to him. I immediately searched my files to locate the copy of the letter I had from fifteen years previously. When I showed that copy to Ms. Dunn, she confirmed that yes, this was the letter that was being donated to Southeast.

A week later, I traveled to Ste. Genevieve to visit Mrs. Parker and to personally thank her for the donation of the letter to the Faulkner Center. In a taped interview, she shared with me the information she knew about her Missouri ancestors, and I told her what I knew of the Mississippi Falkners. Thus a personal quest that began fifteen years earlier now came to a successful and happy, if unexpected, conclusion.

At the time that Southeast acquired the Brodsky Collection, the University Archives—founded and supervised by the History Department—was primarily a repository for school yearbooks, issues of the student newspaper, and Faculty Senate minutes. With the acquisition of the Brodsky Collection, however, the university now owned one of the world's four largest collections of William Faulkner materials. As a result, the university would need to hire its first professional archivist to catalog and oversee the Brodsky Collection.

We found the perfect individual for the job. Dr. Lisa Speer, who had previous experience in working with the Faulkner collection at the University of Mississippi, accepted the position of Head of Special Collections and Archives; and over the next several years she worked with L.D. and me in identifying, cataloging, preserving, and filing the materials in the Brodsky Collection. Her presence on campus, along with the attendant publicity related to the Faulkner collection, led to the acquisition of additional collections: for example, the Houck papers (the personal files of Louis Houck, lawyer, historian, railroad builder, and community leader); the records of the Little River Drainage District Corporation (the organization that directed the construction of the drainage system that opened up the Missouri Bootheel swamp land for agriculture); and the photographs of the Lueders Photographic Studio.

Dr. Speer left Southeast in 2013 to become director of the Arkansas State Archives, located in Little Rock; but her successor, Roxanne Dunn, has continued to expand the holdings of Southeast's Special Collections. Dan Back's huge collection of books on Mississippi River history, the Jo Ann Emerson Congressional papers, the Lida Mayo book collection, and the bird drawings and journals of former SEMO professor Jim Hamby are only the most notable of several acquisitions that Ms. Dunn has arranged for the Archives.

Without a full-time archivist, it is almost certain the materials obtained under the leadership of Dr. Speer and Ms. Dunn wouldn't have been donated to Southeast, and without the Brodsky Collection Southeast would not have had a full-time archivist. Thus the Brodsky Collection and its resultant Faulkner Center have benefitted the university quite beyond their focal role in Faulkner studies.

The Theft

There are high points and low points in any human endeavor, and the lowest of the lows in my work with the Brodsky Collection occurred on November 11, 2002.

On that day I was informed by Dr. Speer, head of Special Collections, that she had received a call from Tom Fisk—a New Haven, Connecticut, book collector—inquiring if a letter then being offered for sale on eBay was from the Brodsky Collection. He was familiar with the Brodsky–Hamblin volumes, and he thought he remembered this letter as having been published in one of our books.

I immediately logged onto the eBay site and quickly scrolled through the Faulkner items. And there it was—a scanned copy of a handwritten letter Faulkner had written to Saxe Commins, his editor, from Cairo, Egypt, in 1951, during the filming of *Land of the Pharaohs*. It was indeed a letter from the Brodsky Collection, and it was supposed to be in our Rare Book Room, not being sold by eBay.

Continuing my search on eBay, I discovered that two additional letters from the Brodsky Collection had already been sold. All three of the letters had been posted on eBay for auction by a Rowlett, Texas, book dealer whom I had never heard of before. I was shocked to find the letters on eBay, the more so since I periodically check the site for Faulkner items but somehow had overlooked these listings.

My mind began racing with all kinds of wild thoughts about how this might have happened. Who could have possibly stolen the letters? Some student during a class visit to the Rare Book Room? One of my graduate research assistants? A visiting research scholar? Was the theft done recently, or had the letters been taken earlier and were only now being disposed of? Our security alarm system was in good working order and frequently tested, and only three people were authorized to open the Rare Book Room—the director of Kent Library, Dr. Speer, and I—so how could someone have taken anything without our knowledge?

The most agonizing thought that entered my mind was that I must call L.D. and inform him of the theft before he heard or read about it in news reports. He had entrusted his marvelous collection with us, and now we had allowed someone to steal a part of it. How could I explain that to him? And what would be his response? I was about to make the hardest phone call I had ever made in my entire life.

I called L.D. and told him what had happened but we didn't yet know the whom or the how. He listened calmly as I nervously explained the situation, and then he spoke. "How's Lisa doing?" he asked with his first words, referring to Dr. Speer, whose responsibility it was, as head of Special Collections, to oversee the Rare Book Room. "She's devastated," I told him, to which he responded, "Tell her everything will be okay."

By this time in our relationship I had already come to know L.D. as a sensitive, caring individual, but his expressed concern for Dr. Speer in this moment of crisis elevated his magnanimity to an even higher and astonishing level. How different was L.D.'s initial reaction from that of one of the university administrators, whose first words, angrily shouted, were, "How in the hell did this happen?"

After a rush of meetings involving school officials, campus security representatives, Dr. Speer, and me, Detective Kenneth Mayberry of our campus police force was put in charge of the investigation. Dr. Speer and I provided him with a list of recent visitors to the Rare Book Room. In addition to student groups and a visiting Japanese scholar, an individual who had signed in as "R. Smith" had viewed the Brodsky Collection on September 30. Dr. Speer also assisted Detective Mayberry in creating a computerized portrait of Smith as she remembered him.

Mayberry quickly contacted the book dealer, Noble Enterprises of Rowlett, Texas, the seller of the letters on eBay, who reported that he obtained the letters from a grocery clerk who claimed to have inherited them from his grandmother's estate. Noble also provided Mayberry with a cell phone number that the seller of the documents had left with the dealer.

Noble said he acquired six Faulkner letters in all; he still had four of them in his possession. The two letters that had sold were purchased, respectively, by a businessman in Oxford—Faulkner's hometown—and a Faulkner collector in Portland, Maine. Both cooperated fully with investigators, relinquishing the letters, and the dealer reimbursed them for the money they had spent to acquire the items.

The Oxford businessman, a Mr. Cooper, had purchased a letter that Faulkner had written to Mrs. Winslow Chapman, the secretary of Longreen Hunt, a fox-hunting club in Germantown, near Memphis, that Faulkner belonged to. Cooper had already had the letter framed, and it was displayed on his office desk when Mayberry went to retrieve it.

The Portland book collector, Seth Berner, is an acquaintance of both Brodsky and me. A frequent exhibitor at the annual Faulkner and Yoknapatawpha Conference, Seth is an authority on not only Faulkner but also many other modern authors. He paid Noble $1,200 for a typed letter that Faulkner sent to Lamar Trotti, the producer of the 1943 film classic, *The Ox Bow Incident*. Berner was drawn to the letter by Faulkner's sensitive comments on the work of another artist. "It's a really shining statement about what art means, made by somebody who made as striking a contribution to literary art as anyone in American letters," Berner told the reporter who interviewed him about his return of the letter.

Berner, of course, was heartsick to learn that the letter he had purchased had been stolen. It was the first time he had ever purchased such an item, he said, adding, "Had I had any clue whatsoever it might have been stolen, I would have not gotten involved in it."

Seth was also very unhappy, understandably so, that I had not given him advance notice that the Portland police would be coming to his bookshop to retrieve the letter. He felt we had needlessly placed him in a very embarrassing situation. I explained that at that point we didn't know whether or not the seller of the eBay items and the thief were one and the same person. Had Seth called the seller asking for his money back, and had that seller also been the thief, we feared that he might have been tempted to destroy any additional evidence he still had in his possession. Fortunately, Seth understood our situation and turned his letter over to a Portland police officer for return to our university. I'm happy to add that, these years later, Seth and I are still friends.

"R. Smith" turned out to be Robert Hardin Smith of Jacksonville, Arkansas, near Little Rock. A former lawyer who had been disbarred several years earlier for defrauding a client, Smith had quite a history of stealing rare documents from university libraries. He had previously been convicted of the 1996 theft of historic letters from the University of Kansas, including three signed by William Quantrill, the Civil War-era guerrilla fighter. He also was convicted of stealing manuscripts from the University of Arkansas, serving nearly three years in prison for that crime before being paroled in 1999. He also had stolen documents from the University of Alabama and the University of Memphis. We later learned that the latter school had a sting operation in place to catch him at the time of his arrest for the Southeast Missouri robbery.

As I told one interviewer following Smith's arrest, "He was a smart thief but a dumb crook." He was experienced and savvy enough to exit the Rare Book Room with the letters, even though an archivist was with him in the room at all times. But he used his own cell phone to make the appointment to view the Brodsky Collection, and he signed in using his actual name. Within twenty-four hours, Detective Mayberry and his staff had solved the crime.

The capture and arrest of the thief, however, took a while longer. Morley Swingle, the Cape Girardeau County prosecuting attorney, who coincidentally is a novelist himself and a professed fan of Faulkner—and who told a reporter that he was "the perfect prosecutor for this case" and would prosecute it "with sound and fury"—quickly issued a warrant for Smith's arrest. However, when the announcement of the warrant was sent from his office to area newspapers, the culprit's name and address were not deleted, as is normally the practice. As a result, a St. Louis reporter, seeking a scoop, I presume, called Smith to interview him. Thus alerted that there was a warrant out for his arrest, Smith ran, and it took law enforcement officials more than a week to find him.

Smith was returned to Cape Girardeau for incarceration and indictment, and Swingle did indeed aggressively prosecute the case. Smith confessed to the crime and, being a second-time offender, was given a seven-year sentence.

There was one interesting footnote to the story of the Faulkner theft. The Texas book dealer informed Detective Mayberry that he had also purchased two John F. Kennedy letters from Smith. Mayberry asked me where the Kennedy letters might belong. I told him to secure photocopies of the letters and I would see what I could find out.

The Kennedy letters were handwritten and addressed to Senator John Stennis of Mississippi. The letters described military actions that the president and Secretary of Defense Robert McNamara were planning to take in Vietnam. Stennis was being notified of the plans because he was then Chairman of the Armed Services Committee.

When I saw that the letters were written to John Stennis, I concluded that the letters had in all likelihood been taken from a Stennis archive, and a quick check of library resources revealed that the Stennis papers were housed at Mississippi State University in Starkville. I enlisted the help of Dr. Speer and Carl Pracht, a Southeast librarian, who called the Mississippi State University Archives to see if they were missing any documents. Not to their knowledge, they said, but Smith had visited their archives recently.

The two Kennedy letters were returned to Mississippi State. No public announcement was ever made about that theft and recovery.

One year after Smith's conviction and imprisonment, Josh Flory, a reporter for the *Columbia Daily Tribune*, published a two-page article based on his interview with Smith in the Moberly Correctional Center in Missouri. In that interview, Smith discussed his long history of document theft, claiming to have stolen more than one hundred documents from several different institutions. He explained to the reporter his method of operation.

Sometimes, Smith said, he would request photocopies of documents in advance and then, when he visited the library, he would secretly swap the copies for the originals. Other times he would simply slip the purloined copies inside his notebook and walk out without being challenged. Sometimes the librarians made it easy for him by leaving him alone with their archives, but even when he was accompanied by an archivist, as at Southeast, he could often still distract the worker long enough to hide documents in his notebook.

All of the librarians that Flory interviewed for his article attested to what a friendly and personable young man Smith was, and the level of trust he created was his principal weapon of deceit. "He was very believable," one said, and another described him as "very innocuous, very nice." All thought he was a person who could be trusted.

After stealing the letters from Southeast, Smith said, he returned to his Arkansas home, hid the letters in his closet, and a few days later sold them to the Texas dealer.

Smith told Flory that he started his career in crime because he was deeply in debt as a result of huge medical bills that he couldn't pay. But he told a fellow inmate in the Cape Girardeau jail (who later shared this information with me) that he was stealing to support a gambling addiction. Of course, both stories could be true.

Smith was released from prison after serving three years of his seven-year sentence. Upon his release, he secured a job working in an abstract office in Springfield, Missouri.

Another Obstacle Overcome

Smith's theft of the Faulkner letters evidences the outside threat that all holders of rare books and manuscripts must be aware of and vigilant to prevent. But one of the biggest threats to the Brodsky Collection came partly from within—and partly from our own doing.

I mentioned earlier that the University Foundation created a revolving fund of $150,000 from which L.D. as curator could borrow (at 8.5 percent interest) to add significant items to the collection by de-acquisitioning other items. That strategy worked wonderfully well at the outset, enabling us to sell or swap a few first editions (the only collectibles that many collectors want) to acquire materials such as manuscripts and letters that would better support scholarly research.

But that practice was sabotaged in 1995 by an incident we had not anticipated.

In 1991, a group of forty-two unpublished letters that Faulkner had written from Hollywood to his family back home in Oxford came on the market, at a price of $155,000. In keeping with our agreed-upon strategy of privileging letters over books, I recommended that we purchase these letters; and L.D. arranged to do so, applying toward the purchase price the balance remaining in the $150,000 revolving account he had with the Foundation. He subsequently contacted a prominent New York bookseller to discuss the sale of books from the collection to cover the debt to the Foundation.

In 1994, after protracted discussions, L.D. and the dealer identified seven books for de-acquisition and agreed to a package deal in which the dealer would acquire the books for a total price of $175,000. The crucial point in the arrangement was the word "package": that is, the purchase price was for the entire lot of seven books, not $25,000 per individual title. L.D. estimated that two or three of the books, including a signed copy of *The Sound and the Fury*, had a market value of $40–50,000 each, while the remaining copies could probably be sold for only $6–12,000 each.

Under heavy pressure from the Foundation to pay back the $150,000 (plus accrued interest) as quickly as possible, and because he trusted the book dealer as a business associate of long standing (they had just completed a transaction a few months previously to the satisfaction of both buyer and seller), L.D. agreed to allow the dealer to pay the $175,000 in quarterly installments over three years. Six such payments were made, but then the dealer returned three of the seven books and defaulted on the remaining payments, totaling $87,500. The three books he returned were the least valuable in the lot.

In defense of his action, the dealer claimed that L.D. had breached the contract by reneging on a promise that he would not offer for sale any more presentation copies from the Brodsky Collection. The dealer had asked for such a pledge because he evidently feared that more signed books on the market would reduce his chances of selling the seven books now in his possession—at least at the prices he planned to ask for them.

As a favor to a friend and longtime business associate, and to enhance the dealer's chances of selling all seven of the books to a single client, L.D. provided a letter describing the provenance of each book and (unwisely, as it turned out) containing the following sentence: "Accordingly, I hereby state that no additional books in the Brodsky Faulkner Collection, inscribed by Faulkner to any of the recipients discussed above, as well as to those recipients of *The Town*, *Sartoris*, and *Sanctuary*, which I previously sold to you, will ever be pulled from my collection or sold to the public." The recipients referred to were John Crown, Joan Williams, Malcolm Franklin, Alabama McLean, Phil Stone, Saxe Commins, Myrtle Ramey, Bill and Victoria Fielden, Hubert Starr, and Edith Brown.

Here is where the matter gets complicated. Not foreseeing that his letter would ever be used for anything other than a bargaining chip with the dealer's client interested in buying all seven of the books, L.D. sold two signed books to another individual. When the dealer learned of this sale, he claimed that the contract he had with L.D. had been broken.

L.D. later explained in a letter to the university's attorney, Joseph J. Russell, that he had written the letter only at the dealer's request and, further, that the ideas and even some of the wording had been dictated to him by the dealer. The letter, L.D. insisted, was intended only as a "selling tool" to be used with a particular client; it was not a part of the contract that he and the dealer had executed. Furthermore, the promise was not to decline to sell *any* signed book in the collection but only those signed to the specified recipients of the books purchased by the dealer.

L.D. went on in his letter to explain to Russell that he had been willing to include the now-troublesome sentence because, had full payment of the $175,000 been made, there would have been enough money to pay off the Foundation debt and thus no further need to sell additional books from the collection. And should that need arise in the future, there were signed books from Faulkner to recipients other than those represented in the contested deal.

Unfortunately for all parties concerned, the buyer that the dealer had in mind declined to take all seven of the books. We never learned how much the dealer received for the four books he did sell, but undoubtedly, given the high quality of the books and inscriptions, it was considerably more than the $87,500 he had already paid Southeast in the quarterly installments.

Only the dealer knows whether he genuinely believed L.D. to be in violation of a contract or whether, once the deal he was working on fell through, he used the technicality of L.D.'s statement as an excuse to void the contract. In any event, the collection owed the Foundation a huge debt and the money we planned to use to pay it off was still in a New York bank account.

There is no doubt, however, concerning L.D.'s feelings on the matter. He concluded the three-page letter to Joe Russell, explaining his involvement in the transaction, with these words: "He is a dishonest man and should be prosecuted to the letter of the law."

The university initiated legal proceedings to collect the balance of the debt; meanwhile, the Foundation instructed L.D. to sell the three books the dealer had returned and apply the proceeds from that sale to the debt owed the Foundation. Just as L.D. had anticipated, those were the least valuable of the books included in the transaction, and their sale netted the Foundation only $28,800. That left the balance of the debt owed to the Foundation at $58,700.

Now the situation got even more complicated. Lawsuits typically move through the courts very slowly, and this one would require Southeast to try the case in New York. Meanwhile, until the case was decided, the Foundation asked L.D. and me to place a moratorium on any further sales from the collection. Yet the interest meter was still ticking against us, upping by the day the money the collection owed to the Foundation.

I can't think of a more stressful time that L.D. and I endured in all the years of our collaboration. The dealer refused to pay the money we thought he owed us, the university was not moving quickly to collect the money, and the applied interest was increasing the amount owed month by month.

Not until 2002 were the issues of this matter finally resolved. And no one was entirely happy with the compromise that effected the resolution. Declining to pursue the case against the dealer in a New York court, the university eventually accepted a $20,000 payment to settle the case. Fortunately for the integrity of the collection, the Foundation agreed to waive the interest charged to the collection after the date of the dealer's forfeiture and the moratorium on additional sales. Finally, and sadly, L.D. and I identified five additional signed books to be sold to clear the remainder of the Foundation debt.

It had been a long, agonizing, near-heartbreaking experience, but now it was over and L.D., I, and the Faulkner Center could re-focus our attention on our primary mission and purpose.

My Favorites

Parents, teachers, and coaches should not play favorites, but research scholars may be allowed that privilege. I've enjoyed all of my involvement with Faulkner and the Brodsky Collection over the years, but I do have my favorite books and projects.

Of all the books and articles that L.D. and I have collaborated on, I most enjoyed our work on *The De Gaulle Story*, the unproduced screenplay that Faulkner wrote for Warner Bros. Studio in 1942. During World War II, Hollywood studios became virtual propaganda agencies turning out films that supported the United States and its allies. Jack Warner, a personal friend of President Roosevelt, was especially dedicated to the war effort; and Faulkner, a Warner employee, was assigned to write a good deal of the propaganda.

Faulkner's *The De Gaulle Story* interweaves the biography of Charles De Gaulle, the leader of the Free French movement, with the stories of two brothers—one a Gaullist and the other a supporter of the Vichy French government, which had condemned De Gaulle to death because he would not sign the French armistice with Germany. De Gaulle escapes to London, where he organizes and commands the underground movement against Hitler and the Germans. In keeping with the patriotic and propagandistic intent of the project, Faulkner's script predicts the eventual victory of the French nation over the German occupation and those who support it.

Even though Faulkner labored diligently on *The De Gaulle Story*, producing some 1,200 pages of manuscript in the various drafts, the film never went into production. There were a number of reasons why: one of the major factors was the conflict that developed between Faulkner and the De Gaulle representatives who served as consultants on the project. Principal among these were Adrien Tixier, a Free French lobbyist in Washington, D.C., and Henri Diamant-Berger, a French film director and producer who was the Gaullist representative in Hollywood. To retrace the exchanges between Faulkner and these

French advisors is to follow a debate on a topic that engaged Faulkner's interest throughout his career—the fundamental conflict between fact and fiction.

In the early stages of his work on *The De Gaulle Story*, Faulkner drew heavily upon Philippe Barres's book, *Charles De Gaulle* (1941), as well as upon various chronologies of events provided by both the Warner Bros. Research Department and the French Research Foundation, a Gaullist front organization located in West Hollywood. Demonstrating his typical disdain for facts, however, Faulkner quickly began to substitute fictional characters and events for the historical details. Given the Free French representatives' loyalty to De Gaulle and their deep commitment to the liberation of France, their response to Faulkner's alterations was predictable.

According to the consultants, Faulkner erred by assigning a Breton peasant family a cook; by having the French play dominoes in cafes; by claiming the general French public had knowledge of De Gaulle's book on tank warfare; and by characterizing De Gaulle's first followers as desperate crowds of beggars and refugees. Moreover, the French army had been on alert in May 1940, and would not have been granting furloughs to soldiers as Faulkner had allowed in his narrative. Additionally, Faulkner had grossly misrepresented De Gaulle's military strategy, and he had placed the general in Syria at a time when he was in France. Further, the consultants argued, the script was wrong in characterizing Bretons as more loyal to their region than to their nation; in describing the roles and behavior of French mayors, constables, and maids; in creating a situation involving forced labor when in fact there had been none; and in anachronistically alluding to announcements over loudspeakers in public places. What bothered the Free French consultants the most, however, was that De Gaulle's role in the script was being steadily diminished as Faulkner focused more and more on the political opposition of the two fictional brothers: Georges, a De Gaulle sympathizer, and Jean, a Vichy collaborator. As Diamant-Berger rightly noted in his critique, "General De Gaulle disappears practically from the story after the first third, and the Fighting French movement with him."

For a time Faulkner sought to placate the French consultants by making many of the changes in the script they requested (although in one instance he could not resist a rejoinder: in response to the notation that the French farmers would be planting potatoes and not corn, Faulkner penciled between the lines: "What does horse eat?"). Finally, exasperated by the unbending, literal mindedness of the Free Frenchmen and recognizing the impasse as having become insurmountable, Faulkner petitioned Robert Buckner, the producer, for a free hand in structuring the screenplay. "Let's dispense with General De Gaulle as a living character in the story," Faulkner wrote in an interoffice memo. The problem, as Faulkner stated it, was that the Frenchmen wanted to produce "a document" rather than "a story." As a consequence, they would continue to "insist upon an absolute adherence to time and fact, no matter how trivial the incident nor imaginary the characters acting it, and regardless of the sacrifice of dramatic values and construction or the poetic implications or overtones." Only by overruling the Frenchmen's demands, Faulkner insisted, could the filmmakers "gain the freedom to make a picture which the American audience whose money will pay for it will understand and not find dull."

Faulkner's pleas, however, went unheeded, and shortly thereafter the studio abandoned its plan to produce a movie about General De Gaulle and the Free French movement. But the story of *The De Gaulle Story* was not finished.

Less than a year after Warner Bros. abandoned *The De Gaulle Story*, director/producer Howard Hawks persuaded the studio to produce a movie version of Ernest Hemingway's 1937 novel, *To Have and Have Not*. Hawks secured a well-known scriptwriter, Jules Furthman, to write the initial draft of the proposed screenplay, but when Furthman left the project to work on another film, Hawks enlisted Faulkner to revise Furthman's work.

To Have and Have Not, both in Hemingway's novel and Furthman's initial script, presents the story of Harry Morgan, a ne'er-do-well who survives during the Great Depression by using his charter boat to smuggle liquor, illegal immigrants, and Cuban revolutionaries between Cuba and Key West. What Faulkner brought to the project, as a result of his recent work on *The De Gaulle Story*, was the notion to recast Hemingway's story as a World War II drama depicting the conflict between the Free French and the Vichy French, the same conflict that had divided the two brothers Georges and Jean in *The De Gaulle Story*. To support this reinterpretation, Hawks shifted the setting of *To Have and Have Not* from Cuba to the island of Martinique, a French province under the control of the Vichy government. This recasting of Hemingway's novel produced two significant effects, one dramatic and one practical. In Faulkner's handling of the story, Morgan, by giving his life in support of the Free French, is presented with a means of moral redemption. In addition, the shift of focus enabled Humphrey Bogart, who played the part of Harry Morgan, to reprise the Free French role that had been such a success in the recent Warner Bros. production of *Casablanca* (1942).

Readers and critics did not know how much *The De Gaulle Story* influenced the making of the film *To Have and Have Not* until L.D. and I co-edited Faulkner's De Gaulle screenplay for publication in 1984 by the University Press of Mississippi as Volume III of *Faulkner: A Comprehensive Guide to the Brodsky Collection*. Since we included not only the completed screenplay but also the progressive versions from original story treatment to the revised script, as well as the studio's file materials relating to the project, the volume provided for the first time a fairly complete record, from beginning to end, of Faulkner's work on a single movie project. Brodsky and I co-authored an introduction to the volume that traces the history of Faulkner's work on the project and offers some conclusions about the merits of the script and the reasons it was never filmed. Brodsky and I believed then, and continued to believe, that *The De Gaulle Story* clearly dispels the popular myth (frequently advanced by Faulkner himself) that Faulkner never really took screenwriting seriously and engaged in the work solely for the money. The truth is that Faulkner worked extremely hard in Hollywood and eventually became a more than competent, if not outstanding, scriptwriter.

The positive critical response to the publication of *The De Gaulle Story* indicated that most scholars and readers were pleased that a Faulkner work, even one that is definitely inferior to the great fiction, had finally been published after lying dormant for so many years. But one individual took great offense to the appearance of the book. Catherine Gavin, a British historian, wrote me a personal letter, claiming that much of the new material that Brodsky and I presented in our introduction was "rubbish" and questioning whether the publication of Faulkner's script was a late attempt to revive and defend Gaullist politics. She concluded as follows:

> Owing no doubt to some oversight of the editors,
> your name does not appear in *Who's Who in America*,
> so I have no idea of your age. Are you one of the
> new breed of academics, eager for publicity, in your
> case by climbing on the Gaullist bandwagon even
> at this late date? Or were you an adult in 1940? I

was, and on June 18, 1940, I listened to de Gaulle's first mendacious broadcast on the BBC. I have been his enemy, through life and death, from that hour onwards.

Fortunately, other critics and reviewers were less emotionally involved, less hostile, and more grateful.

For the final segment of the history of *The De Gaulle Story*, the setting shifts from the United States to France. In 1989, Faulkner's French publisher, Éditions Gallimard, issued a French translation of the Mississippi Press volume Brodsky and I had prepared. Yannick Guillou, a representative of Gallimard, had initially contacted Brodsky about a possible French translation shortly after learning of the pending publication of the American edition. Gallimard's interest was significantly heightened after a five-page feature story about Faulkner's rediscovered script appeared in *L'Express*, the French news weekly. François Forestier, the author of that story, had traveled to the United States to interview not only Brodsky and me but also Buzz Bezzerides and other of Faulkner's 1940s Hollywood acquaintances.

The interest of both Gallimard and *L'Express* in Faulkner's script about the former French general and president was undoubtedly governed more by political and historical than by literary motives, since the appearance of both the book and the article coincided with the plans of the French nation to celebrate, in 1990, the one hundredth anniversary of De Gaulle's birth and the fiftieth anniversary of the beginning of De Gaulle's resistance movement from London. In conjunction with this nationwide celebration, TF1, a French television network, announced plans to produce a 20 million franc television movie based on Faulkner's script. Bertrand Poirot-Delpech, a well-known literary columnist, was employed to adapt Faulkner's script for the screen; and Henri Serre, a noted French actor, was enlisted to play the role of De Gaulle. The film was released under the title *Moi, General De Gaulle* and telecast in November 1990. Most reviewers concluded that the movie was not very good; moreover, it varied significantly from Faulkner's original script. Still, although in an altered state, Faulkner's story of De Gaulle and the Free French had finally made its way to the screen. Thus concluded, in France, a story that had had its beginning nearly fifty years earlier in Hollywood.

Turning to Faulkner's novels, I find it very difficult to pick a favorite. In little more than a decade from 1929 until 1942, Faulkner produced nine novels, five of which (*The Sound and the Fury*, *As I Lay Dying*, *Light in August*, *Absalom, Absalom!*, and *Go Down, Moses*) have been touted by one critic or another as his greatest novel. When you think about it, it is remarkable that critics cannot reach a consensus on which of those books is Faulkner's masterpiece. Mention Nathaniel Hawthorne and you think of *The Scarlet Letter*; Melville, *Moby Dick*; Twain, *Adventures of Huckleberry Finn*. But critics can reach no agreement on Faulkner. It's like trying to decide which of Shakespeare's tragedies or Beethoven's symphonies is the creator's greatest.

I'm fond of *As I Lay Dying* because it's the novel that got me hooked on Faulkner, and I think *The Sound and the Fury* is a world classic, and I find the major characters in *Light in August* to be remarkable, and I believe "The Bear" in *Go Down, Moses* contains some of the finest prose in the English language. But my choice for Faulkner's greatest novel, and thus my favorite, is *Absalom, Absalom!*

It has taken *Absalom, Absalom!* quite a long time to climb to or near the top of Faulkner's rankings. The *New York Times* still doesn't include it in the list of 100 greatest novels, although three other Faulkner novels (*The Sound and the Fury*, *As I Lay Dying*, and *Light in August*) make the list. An early satirical review by influential literary critic Clifton Fadiman (in the October 31, 1936, issue of *The New Yorker*) didn't help the case for *Absalom, Absalom!*

Fadiman opens his essay by saying that Quentin Compson's statements in the novel—"You can't understand it [the South]. You would have to be born there"—are not only among "the few comprehensible sentences in the entire novel but also beyond a doubt the truest." Fadiman continues: "One may sum up both substance and style by saying that every person in *Absalom, Absalom!* comes to no good end, and they all take a hell of a time coming even that far." Faulkner's style, Fadiman claims, is characterized by "the Non-Stop or Life Sentence," "the Far Fetch, or Hypertrope," and "Anti-Narrative, a set of complex devices used to keep the story from being told." Regarding Faulkner's use of multiple narrators, Fadiman says that Faulkner "tears the Sutpen chronicle into pieces, as if a mad child were to go to work on it with a pair of shears." Faulkner's plot is nothing more than "the melodramatic gestures of childish maniacs" who are candidates for "a literary asylum for the feeble-minded." All that Faulkner accomplishes, Fadiman concludes, is "a neat job of mixing up the time sequences, delaying climaxes, confusing the reader, and . . . demonstrating that as a technician he has Joyce and Proust punch-drunk."

Humorous it is, but Fadiman's review represents a complete misunderstanding of Faulkner's great novel. In fact, the very elements that Fadiman ridicules are the features that make *Absalom* a masterpiece.

Absalom, Absalom! presents the tragic story of Thomas Sutpen, a Southerner who rises from poverty to become a wealthy plantation owner, only to see his dream of a family dynasty collapse as a result of the Civil War and the racial conflict within his own family. However, as is so often the case with a Faulkner novel, it is not the story that is told so much as the manner of the telling that accounts for the novel's greatness.

The principal events of the Sutpen story take place between 1807 and 1869; however, Faulkner chooses to present the events as they are recollected and interpreted forty years later, in 1909–10, by a varied group of narrators, principally a young college student, Quentin Compson. Since all but the denouement of the Sutpen story has taken place before Quentin's birth, he must depend on others for the bulk of his information, compiling the narrative "out of the rag-tag and bob-ends of old tales and talking." The general outline of the Sutpen story Quentin knows, as all Jeffersonians do, "from having been born and living beside it, with it," but the specific details come to him from his father (who in turn has much of his information from his father), from Miss Rosa Coldfield, Sutpen's sister-in-law, and finally, at the very end, from Sutpen's son Henry. Since none of his sources knows the complete Sutpen story (and much they presume to know is based on hearsay), and since each of these separate accounts reflects a particular set of opinions and even biases, Quentin must deduce the complete story and its meaning from the multiple accounts. Thus he becomes a kind of detective, following various clues, listening to different testimonies, and trying to piece together the numerous story fragments into a coherent, cohesive whole.

But Faulkner still has one more twist to add to the narrative. In the second half of the novel, he introduces another narrator, Shreve McCannon, a Canadian who is Quentin's Harvard roommate, who adds his own speculation and imaginative interpretation to Quentin's account of the events. By this stage of the novel, Thomas Sutpen has practically ceased to be a historical figure, even one presented through rumor and hearsay, and has become a figment of Quentin's and Shreve's imagination. In short, history, or presumed history, has become fiction.

One way that Faulkner dramatizes the uncertainty and ambiguity of inherited "facts" is by attributing at various points of the narrative differing theories of the motive for Henry Sutpen's murder of Charles Bon to prevent Bon from marrying Henry's sister Judith. As Joseph Warren Beach, an early reviewer more sympathetic to Faulkner's technique than Fadiman, commented, "Faulkner keeps the reader for hundreds of pages barking up the wrong tree, and then a second wrong tree, while all the time his real game is lodged in the branches of a third." To Miss Rosa, the reason for Henry's objection to the marriage of Judith and Bon is an unfathomable mystery, explicable only by its association with Thomas Sutpen, the man she is persuaded is a "demon." Mr. Compson thinks the threat of bigamy is the reason, based on Henry's discovery of Bon's octoroon mistress and child in New Orleans. Next, the reader is led to believe that the protestation results from the revelation that Bon is Sutpen's son from a previous marriage, thus introducing the threat of incest as the reason for Henry's opposition. Only at the end of the novel is the "true" motive revealed—the "fact" that Bon is part-Negro and Henry cannot tolerate the threatened miscegenation. Even here, however, Faulkner refuses to present this final revelation in absolute terms, as the reader cannot be totally sure whether this is the real motive or only the one invented by Quentin and Shreve in their imaginative reconstruction of the story.

And herein lies the ultimate greatness of this great novel. What is truth? Can actual facts ever be separated from our personal perspective—indeed, from our own opinions, desires, and prejudices? Similarly, what is history? Is it a set of ascertainable events, behaviors, and motives, or is a social construct of those who come afterward and reconstruct the past to fit their own needs and circumstances? Or is truth, personal or historical, both of these things—a double-edged phenomenon that is partly objective, partly subjective; partly actual, partly imagined?

Faulkner knew that humankind is the myth-making animal. While this quality can be turned to good effect—as in the creation of art and idealistic dreams of a better world—it can also have disastrous consequences. Faulkner grew up in a place and time that rationalized and excused chattel slavery and notions of white supremacy, and glorified the "Lost Cause" of the antebellum South and the Confederacy. In this world, there were many voices demanding attention and allegiance, and among the most dangerous were the absolutists, those who never examined, much less questioned, their own beliefs and values and, not unlike Thomas Sutpen, sought to impose their views on others.

Our world, of course, is no different. Myriads of voices speak to us, each offering its absolutist view of beliefs, values, and behaviors:

talk radio hosts, television commentators, politicians, economists, evangelical fundamentalists, Zionists, jihadists, gun owners and opponents, pro-life and pro-choice advocates, leftists and rightists— all loudly and too often intolerantly insisting that they are right and everybody else is wrong.

Absalom, Absalom!, with its epistemological questioning of knowledge and truth, is a cautionary tale warning each of us to be a bit more humble in our convictions and our expression of them. The danger of hubris, or pride, is a theme of much great literature, from Sophocles to Shakespeare to Melville's Captain Ahab; and it is, for good reason, the first in the Catholic Church's list of the cardinal sins. Thus it would seem that a degree of skepticism about all held beliefs and actions might be not only the beginning of tolerance and peace but even of wisdom. Such, I believe, is a major lesson we can learn from *Absalom, Absalom!*

Some Personal Rewards

People are surprised to learn that William Faulkner is not my favorite author. I prefer poets to prose writers, and among the poets my favorites are Shakespeare, Robert Frost, and Emily Dickinson. Among contemporaries, I especially admire and enjoy Seamus Heaney, Stephen Dunn, Billy Collins, and Natasha Trethewey.

It might seem the height of ingratitude to say, as a writer, that I'd rather be a Frost or a Dickinson (Shakespeare being out of the question) than a Faulkner—the more so since Faulkner has done so much for me, both personally and professionally. He has carried me, both literally and figuratively, around the world.

One of my most gratifying experiences has been my involvement in the "Teaching Faulkner" sessions at the annual Faulkner and Yoknapatawpha Conference at Ole Miss. Recognizing that the conference needed to pay more acknowledgment to classroom teachers and their teaching of Faulkner's novels and stories, Ann Abadie, the co-director of the conference, asked me to chair an exploratory session on "Teaching Faulkner" at the 1989 conference. Those sessions have since become a staple of the annual conference and are among the most popular of the activities, but they didn't get off to the best of starts.

Conference participants in the early days had grown accustomed to hearing academics read papers at the sessions, so when they came to the first "Teaching Faulkner" session, they were expecting another formal presentation. However, I had prepared no formal remarks, choosing instead to involve the teachers in general discussion about the issues, strategies, challenges, and rewards of using Faulkner's novels and stories in the classroom. Moreover, I anticipated having only twenty-five to thirty people attend the session, and I planned to do some small-group work in discussing the various topics. To my surprise, more than one hundred people showed up for the session, which was held in one of the mock courtrooms in the Ole Miss law building—where, as I quickly noticed, every chair in the room was bolted to the floor. So there I was, with no prepared speech, a larger-than-expected audience that was conditioned to listening rather than speaking, no way to circle the chairs into small groups, and no microphone. It appeared that we were going to have a very short session!

Even today, these many years later, I credit Sister Mary Dolorine Pires with saving my life that awkward day. At that time Sister Mary, a Sacred Heart nun, was teaching Faulkner novels and stories in her classes at the American University in Rome, and she broke the ice by sharing some of her experiences in teaching Faulkner's works to the international students enrolled in her classes. After her comments, others joined in, and, despite the logistical problems, we actually had a pretty good session—successful enough to suggest that a Teaching Faulkner session should be included in the next conference.

For that conference, fearful of repeating my near failure of the year before, I invited Jim Carothers of the University of Kansas to assist me in leading the discussion. Jim is not only an outstanding Faulkner scholar but also a great humorist, and I knew he could salvage any disaster with a good dose of levity. It was a partnership that would last for almost twenty years. Jim is fond of saying that those sessions we chaired attracted "more participants than any activity at the conference that didn't involve food and drink."

The second Teaching Faulkner session went exceedingly well, and, in succeeding years as the sessions grew in popularity, we added, first, Charles A. Peek of Kearney State University in Nebraska and Arlie Herron of the University of Tennessee–Chattanooga to our leadership team and, later, Theresa Towner of the University of Texas at Dallas and Terrell Tebbetts of Lyon College in Arkansas. Arlie and I have since dropped out of the lineup, but the others—along with newcomer Brian McDonald, an AP teacher from Lancaster, Pennsylvania—continue, and the Teaching Faulkner sessions remain one of the most popular (and I think most valuable) activities of the annual conference.

The lasting friendships have been one of the greatest rewards of the Teaching Faulkner sessions. Jim Carothers and his wife, Beverly, are counted in that number. Jim, a native of St. Louis, is also a close personal friend of L.D. Brodsky, and when Southeast Missouri State University hosted a program celebrating the twenty-fifth anniversary of the Brodsky and Hamblin collaboration, Jim was the invited speaker at the event.

Chuck Peek and his wife, Nancy, are other dear friends whose friendship has deepened over the years. The collaboration Chuck and I began in the Teaching Faulkner sessions continued in our co-editing of two books—*A William Faulkner Encyclopedia* and *A Critical Companion to William Faulkner*. I've delivered guest lectures on his campus, and he on mine. In addition to being an English professor, Chuck is an Episcopal priest and a fine poet—his *Breezes on Their Way to Being Winds* claimed the poetry prize in the 2016 Nebraska Book Awards competition. I've benefitted greatly from Chuck's spiritual insights and advice over the course of our friendship.

Sister Mary Dolorine, who bailed me out in that first session, has become one of our dearest friends. Kaye and I have visited her in Rome and, following her retirement from teaching, in her native state of Hawaii; she has visited us on several occasions in Cape Girardeau. She was one of the researchers who helped document the eligibility of Father Damien, the Hawaiian "leper priest," for sainthood; and Kaye and I celebrated with her, though at long distance, on the day of his beatification. During my writing of *Dust and Light*, a book of poems based on the life and works of Pierre Teilhard de Chardin, Sister Mary pointed me to a number of individuals who helped me in my study and understanding of Teilhard's life and work. One of my favorite poems describes one of Sister Mary's visits with us, and one of the poems in *Dust and Light* is dedicated to her.

I mentioned previously the three National Endowment for the Humanities seminars that I directed in the 1980s. Entitled "William Faulkner: The Regional and the Mythic," these seminars examined the way Faulkner fused characters, stories, and scenes from his native Mississippi with older stories from the Bible and other classical sources to create a literature of lasting and universal significance.

For each of the three summer seminars, fifteen secondary teachers from across the nation were selected to participate, and one or two teachers from an overseas country were added to each group. In total, teachers from thirty-five American states and three foreign countries participated in the seminars, which remain among the highlights of my teaching career.

The first two seminars met the first five weeks on the campus of Southeast Missouri State University and spent the last week at the annual Faulkner and Yoknapatawpha Conference at the University of Mississippi. We traveled to Farmington to visit with L.D. Brodsky and talk with him about his longtime interest in Faulkner. In our breaks from our Faulkner studies, we went sightseeing in St. Louis, visited Mark Twain's hometown of Hannibal, and took a float trip on the Current River. We also set aside one evening each week for the teachers from various parts of the country, and from private as well as public schools, to compare and contrast issues and practices in their respective schools.

For the third year of the seminar, Ann Abadie of the Center for the Study of Southern Culture at Ole Miss invited me to move the entire six-week seminar to Ole Miss. She arranged housing for us in one of the sorority houses that was unoccupied during the summer, and made other university programs and facilities available to us. While I was pleased that those teachers would have more time to immerse themselves in the history and culture of Faulkner's hometown and region (including a weekend trip to New Orleans), I still regret that that group missed out on SEMO, Cape Girardeau, St. Louis, and the Current River.

All of us involved in those seminars made some great friends and shared a number of memorable experiences. There was even one marriage that resulted from the seminars. Jim Nicholson of Kentucky and Leita Nicholson from California fell in love that summer and were married in the fall. In acknowledgment of Faulkner's role in bringing them together, they included in their ceremony the wedding hymn, "The Voice That Breathed O'er Eden," which plays a significant role in the Quentin section of *The Sound and the Fury*. And they invited their seminar director to the wedding.

For one of our float trips, Doug Pokorny—a former student of mine, a high school English teacher in Piedmont, Missouri, and a participant in the seminar—offered the services of one of his friends, an experienced canoeist, to guide us down the river. Not being much of a canoeist myself, I gladly accepted Doug's offer.

After we rented our canoes, hauled them to the river, and unloaded them from the trailers, we gathered on the bank of the river preparing for the start of our grand adventure. Since several of the seminar participants were city folks who had never ridden in a canoe before, I asked Doug's friend if he had any advice for the group before we started out. I was shocked when he said, "I've never been in a canoe in my entire life."

When I turned to Doug for an explanation, he said, "The other friend couldn't come. So I asked Jack."

Having to move on without any advice from Jack, we selected partners, climbed into the canoes, and headed downstream. Jack was paired with Marjorie Shoaf of Florida, an experienced water sporter.

But before their canoe had covered the first hundred yards, Jack had managed to capsize their boat twice, dumping both riders and all their gear into the river.

I waved Pokorny and his partner to the bank and ordered Jack into the canoe with Pokorny. For the rest of the day we all watched Doug and Jack float blissfully down the river, drinking beer, seldom using their paddles, their canoe floating totally out of control, sometimes going forward, sometimes backward, and twisting and turning in the rapids. But at least Marjorie had been saved from drowning.

At one of the Faulkner conferences, my NEH group expressed surprise and disappointment that there was no conference t-shirt. I explained that the Faulkner family opposed commercialization of the Faulkner name in any form, and the conference organizers had complied with the family's request. But my group decided they wanted a t-shirt to commemorate their time together, and they enlisted the artist in our group, Betty Kort of Hastings, Nebraska, to design one. Betty elected to put Faulkner's map of Yoknapatawpha on the front and a quotation from *The Sound and the Fury* on the back. The quote is Faulkner's famous tribute to African Americans for surviving their tragic history, but I'm fairly positive that Betty also intended the statement as an inside joke at the expense of the seminar director: the quote read, "They endured."

When our group showed up at the conference picnic at Rowan Oak wearing our matching shirts, everybody flocked around us to inquire where they could get one of the shirts. But the seminar group would have none of that, instructing Betty to inform the Oxford merchant who produced the shirts for us not to print and sell any additional copies.

But the following year, as every year since, the Faulkner and Yoknapatawpha Conference has issued an official t-shirt for all participants. I purchased a few of those over the years, but the one I most cherish (and still possess) is the 1985 one, the very first Faulkner t-shirt ever seen at the annual conference.

In 1987, when my NEH group spent the entire six weeks at Ole Miss, some of the group, led by Michael Rieman of Brooklyn, New York, became involved in local politics. One of Faulkner's grand-nephews was running for a county office. Michael decided that, as a tribute to the subject of our seminar, we should support his relative's campaign by handing out his candidate cards and flyers on the town square. I warned Michael that historically the Faulkner family had not been very popular with many people in Oxford, and I doubted that the sentiment had changed very much. But Michael and his helpers were not to be dissuaded. They walked the square day after day, promoting their candidate.

There were twelve candidates in the race. The one named Faulkner finished tenth. Had it not been for the campaigning of my NEHers on his behalf, I'm persuaded, he most likely would have finished twelfth.

Another highlight in my teaching of Faulkner came in 2005, with the opportunity to lead the discussion of *As I Lay Dying* for the Oprah Book Club during Oprah Winfrey's "Summer of Faulkner." That was a joyful and rewarding experience, but one that I came very close to missing out on.

One day in March of that year, I returned from teaching a class to find a message on my office phone. It was an invitation to participate in an "educational survey," and I was about to delete the message and hang up when I heard the word "Oprah." Now curious, I returned the call.

Mercedes Carlton, a representative of the Oprah Book Club, explained that she had some news that she thought I'd be interested in, but before she could tell me, I'd have to sign a confidentiality agreement. So the next hour we spent exchanging faxes, and once Mercedes had received my signed agreement that I would not disclose the contents of our conversation to anyone, she explained that I was being invited to teach one of the three Faulkner novels that would be read in the coming weeks by the Oprah Book Club. Since I was the first professor to be contacted, I could have my choice of the novels: *As I Lay Dying*, *The Sound and the Fury*, or *Light in August*. I chose *As I Lay Dying*, largely because I thought that novel would be easier to deal with in the short preparation time I would have.

Mercedes also asked me to supply the names of ten other Faulkner scholars whom I would recommend for the Oprah project. She suggested I not list any academics whose approach might be "over the heads" of the general readers who represent the majority of the Oprah Book Club members.

"Well, you've already got one who qualifies," I joked. "I've never been accused of being over anyone's head."

As requested, I provided a list of Faulkner scholars whom I thought were well suited for the purpose, and soon afterward I was informed that Thadious Davis of the University of Pennsylvania (enlisted to lead the discussion of *The Sound and the Fury*) and Arnold Weinstein of

Brown University (who would lead the study of *Light in August*) would be joining me on the "Summer of Faulkner" team—two scholars from Ivy League schools and one from Southeast Missouri State University. I felt those Ivy Leaguers were fortunate to be associated with SEMO.

On June 3, 2005, on her internationally televised talk show, Oprah Winfrey reached into a huge carton labeled "Big Surprise," pulled out a boxed set of three novels, and announced that William Faulkner would be the featured author for Oprah's Book Club for the next three months. In June, Winfrey explained, the club would read *As I Lay Dying*, in July *The Sound and the Fury*, and in August *Light in August*. Then she posted photographs of the three professors on the screen, identifying us and listing our credentials. Even before the show had ended, my phone was ringing, as former students from across the country began calling to tell me they heard my name mentioned by Oprah.

Within twenty-four hours following Winfrey's announcement of her choice of Faulkner, the boxed set of three Vintage paperbacks climbed to number two on the best-seller list, trailing only J.K. Rowling's announced Harry Potter sequel. Little wonder that Joseph Urgo, then chairman of the English department at the University of Mississippi in Oxford, Faulkner's hometown, called Winfrey's "Summer of Faulkner" "the best thing that's happened to Faulkner since the Nobel Prize."

Naturally I was thrilled to be a part of an endeavor that would introduce Faulkner to legions of new readers. For example, consider this: if only one of every ten of the alleged six hundred thousand members of Oprah's Book Club joined me in reading *As I Lay Dying*, that would still amount to more than seven times the number of students I had taught in my entire teaching career. Oprah's "Faulkner 101" would be by far the largest class I had ever taught!

Like each of the other professors selected to participate in the project, I contracted to videotape a series of short lectures for showing on the oprah.com website (a new lecture being added to the site each week), as well as to post weekly answers to a select number of questions emailed to the oprah.com staff by readers of the novel. I was also commissioned to write an introductory essay offering advice for first-time Faulkner readers. Repeating suggestions I've offered my own students over the years, I recommended that Oprah readers be patient and willing to reread Faulkner's texts, focus on the characters, place the novels within their historical and mythic contexts, and allow for a considerable degree of ambiguity of meaning (and thus multiple interpretations).

Not everyone agreed with Joe Urgo that Winfrey's "Summer of Faulkner" was a good thing. Indeed, I was quite shocked by the degree of opposition and even animosity directed at Winfrey for her choice of Faulkner. If, according to her critics, some of the authors she had previously featured had not been good enough to deserve the attention and fame she heaped upon them, Faulkner, those critics now seemed to be saying, was too good.

Numerous commentators, both popular and academic, questioned whether Oprah's collection of readers—presumably more schooled in talk shows, soap operas, and popular fiction than in high modernist texts—could handle the difficult challenge of reading Faulkner. One internet blogger accused Oprah and her defenders of being "deluded." He continued: "With the American cultural landscape defined these days by Paris Hilton, FOX news, celebrity trials, infotainment, 'Who's Your Daddy' and reality TV in general, there's some notion that the average American is going to appreciate Faulkner? . . . Isn't the attention span of the average American about the length of a *People* magazine article?" Another blogger called me a "professor/whore" for cooperating with Winfrey in what he thought was a misdirected and futile attempt to package Faulkner for mass consumption. The same individual ridiculed the invitation by the oprah.com staff for readers to try their own hand at stream of consciousness narration, noting that such an invitation "assumes a consciousness to stream."

Other observers, however, were less elitist and far more supportive and confident of what Oprah was attempting to do. These individuals typically commended Winfrey for her noble attempt to raise the reading level of the general public. The most noteworthy—and balanced—treatment of this side of the issue was J.R. Tyree's article in the August 1, 2005, issue of *Nation*. Tyree describes Winfrey's choice of Faulkner as "nothing less than a sneak attack on the whole idea of beach reading—and on the intelligentsia's perception of her as the Queen of Midcult." While acknowledging Faulkner to be "a quantum leap up" from Oprah's previous selections, Tyree notes that the choice also represented "an admirably American assertion about the democracy of reading," as well as "[Oprah's] belief in uplift through education." Tyree parallels Oprah's promotion of Faulkner to the days when photographs of great writers such as James Joyce, Faulkner, and Virginia Woolf appeared on the covers of national magazines. Thus, Tyree observes, "Perhaps Oprah's Book Club is making a subtle suggestion that the pendulum has swung too far to the side of anti-intellectualism." In Tyree's view, even if Oprah failed to convince the masses to love Faulkner, her intention and effort were valorous and consistent with the highest ideals of democratic education.

Happily, my being caught up, albeit indirectly, in the culture war debate over Winfrey's celebration of Faulkner was far outweighed by a highly positive benefit I gained from my involvement. I refer here to my developing awareness of, and education in, the process of collaborative reading. While her most extreme critics are loath to admit it, Winfrey is onto something resembling genius in her approach to reading. Part of the success of OBC is undoubtedly due to the admiration and trust Oprah inspires in her followers: because of her great popularity, Oprah's endorsement clearly sells books, as it does other products. But one has only to scan the posts of her readers to recognize that the appeal of the collaborative reading experience that is the hallmark of Oprah's Book Club extends far beyond the influence of a charismatic leader. Even more, in my estimation, it is the interaction of the club members with one another that constitutes the real uniqueness—and the great success—of OBC; and such interaction becomes even more evident and crucial when the author being read is one as difficult as Faulkner. Even in our classrooms, reading remains primarily an individual and private experience—the interaction of a single reader with a particular text. But with the participants in Oprah's Book Club, reading is done by a community, very nearly a family, of readers.

After participating in the OBC's "Summer of Faulkner," I incorporated collaborative reading exercises into all of my literature classes. As a result of this practice, my students became better students and, I am convinced, I became a better teacher.

Along with my teaching activities, my scholarship related to Faulkner has allowed me to partner with a number of outstanding individuals who have also become fast friends. In addition to my work with L.D. Brodsky, I have co-edited Faulkner volumes with Charles Peek, Kearney State University; Stephen Hahn, William Paterson University; Ann Abadie, University of Mississippi; Nicholas Fargnoli, Molloy University; and Melanie Speight and Christopher Rieger, Southeast Missouri State University.

Of this group, Ann Abadie deserves special mention. She and I were graduate students together at Ole Miss, and we have been close friends ever since. As mentioned previously, it was she who invited me to organize and direct the Teaching Faulkner sessions at the Ole Miss conference, as well as to hold my 1987 NEH Summer Seminar on the Ole Miss campus. She also invited me to serve with her as co-editor of the 2000 Faulkner and Yoknapatawpha proceedings, *Faulkner in the Twenty-First Century*. We dedicated that book to our professor and mentor, John Pilkington. In 2013, when the University Press of Mississippi decided to add a Faulkner biography to its series of literary biographies for young and general readers, Ann recommended me to Leila Salisbury, the director of the Press, and Leila invited me to write the book. I hope *Myself and the World: A Biography of William Faulkner*, published in 2016, has not been a disappointment to either of them. One of my other biographies, *Living in Mississippi: The Life and Times of Evans Harrington*, is dedicated to Ann and one of her Ole Miss colleagues, Gerald Walton.

Not the least of my personal rewards in working with Faulkner and Brodsky are the many opportunities I have had to travel throughout the United States and to several foreign countries to teach and lecture on Faulkner. In addition to participating in the Teaching Faulkner sessions, I've delivered five papers at the Faulkner and Yoknapatawpha Conference, the first in 1980, the last in 2016. I spoke at Faulkner's Centennial celebration at his birthplace, New Albany, Mississippi. I spent a delightful week discussing Faulkner with Michael Strelow and his students at Willamette University in Salem, Oregon. I've lectured to Tom Pasko's students in Cleveland, Ohio; Nick Fargnoli's in Rockville Centre, New York; Nancy Blattner's in Caldwell, New Jersey; and Brian McDonald's in Lancaster, Pennsylvania. I've presented papers at conferences sponsored by numerous academic organizations, including the Modern Language Association, the American Culture Association, the Southern Literary Festival, and the Sport Literature Association. I've taught Faulkner seminars and delivered Faulkner lectures in England, the Netherlands, Japan, China, Taiwan, and Romania. In Japan, our host, Nobuaki Namiki of Senshu University, drove Kaye and me to Nagano, where we retraced Faulkner's visit to that city; and Faulkner scholars Hisao Tanaka and Toshio Koyama led us on tours of Hiroshima and Kyoto. In Romania, Didi-Ionel Cenuser, who had previously spent a year at the Faulkner Center as a Fulbright scholar, accompanied us on a week-long driving tour of his native country.

"My, my, how a body does get around," says Lena Grove, as Faulkner takes her from Alabama to Mississippi to Tennessee. He has taken me much, much farther.

Two Poets

Early in our relationship L.D. and I discovered that, despite our very different backgrounds, we had many things in common besides our love of Faulkner's writings. We were both married, with a great love for our families. We had both been "jocks": he played baseball and football for Country Day High School in St. Louis and rowed crew for Yale, and I played baseball and basketball across north Mississippi. We both were liberal Democrats, and we both had broken with the religious upbringing of our youth—for him orthodox Judaism and for me Baptist fundamentalism.

Another interest we shared in common was our love of poetry. We are both published poets, though he is a far better poet than I, as well as a more prolific and more dedicated one. L.D. was already an established poet when I met him, with a dozen chapbooks to his credit and appearances in *Harper's* and other prominent periodicals. I was a "closet" poet, having written a good number of poems but only a few that I had been brave enough to submit for publication.

Almost always when we met to work on our Faulkner projects, our conversation at some point turned to poetry. Often L.D. would read to me his latest poem, and later in our friendship, I would read mine to him. We discussed our favorite poets, and he always wanted to know which poets (and other authors) I was teaching in my literature classes. On our overnight visits these conversations frequently went on far into the night and early morning.

Once the internet and electronic mail became available and popular, L.D. and I had another means with which to keep in touch, and we corresponded often, frequently about the poems we were working on. (The Faulkner projects we typically discussed face-to-face or by telephone.) It was always a great delight for me to open an email, at work or at home, and find the draft of a new poem by L.D. I was always amazed at the volume and the variety of his poetry.

I learned from L.D. most of what I know concerning a poet's

temperament and much of what I know about the poet's craft. The first lesson, taught by both word and example, had to do with dedication. From his late teens throughout his life, L.D. wrote poetry almost every day—more than thirteen thousand poems in all. With the possible exception of Marcel Proust or Walt Whitman, L.D. Brodsky very likely has left behind the most complete record of one individual's existence in all of literature.

L.D. wrote the first drafts of his poems in a large ledger book; there are dozens of them now filled with his handwritten manuscripts. He used a ballpoint pen (always a Bic) and printed the words instead of writing in cursive. The current ledger book was his constant companion. He even wrote in it while driving—pen in hand, the ledger book beside him on the front seat, his eyes watching the road but occasionally glancing down at the page. Even before the advent of cellular phones, he practiced an early form of texting while driving.

I first learned of this writing practice of L.D.'s when I followed his vehicle on a return trip from the University of Missouri at Rolla, which had hosted one of our exhibits. I noticed L.D.'s vehicle drifting erratically ahead of me; I feared he was going to sleep at the wheel. When we stopped for a break, I asked him what was going on. That's when he first demonstrated for me his technique of writing when he was on the road.

When I first met L.D., I was a casual poet, writing only occasionally and when the spirit moved me. I never went looking for poems; I waited for them to come to me. Whatever discipline I had mastered in my life went into my teaching, my scholarly work, and my golf game, but not into my poetry. Observing L.D., I learned how a serious poet works—his constant commitment, dedication, and effort.

In those days, even when a poem came my way, I wouldn't put it on paper until it was pretty well composed in my head. It pains me today to think how many poems may have slipped through my mind and fingers, unrecorded, since poems, no more than any other type of writing, seldom come to one self-contained and complete. They begin with an image, a fleeting thought, a phrase, or a line; and I had been too content to risk holding those in my mind and memory instead of committing them to paper.

L.D.'s constant advice to me was "Trust the process." Get down on paper that image, that thought, that phrase, and be patient in waiting for the rest of the poem to come. Don't be afraid of the blank or half-empty page. Let the imagination work at its own pace.

Under his advice and tutelage, I learned to appreciate more and more the process of making a poem. Looking at the multitudinous drafts of his poems, I became more acutely aware of the origin of a poem and how it grows from beginning to end. In fact, to my surprise, the process of finding and creating a poem became as interesting to me as the finished product. Even a mediocre poem may have a fascinating history.

To cite but one example, my poem "Swoboda"—about Ron Swoboda, the major league baseball player who had played on the high school team in Baltimore for which I served as the assistant coach—was initially left unfinished because I could not settle on an ending. So I filed the fragment away in the folder I keep for poems in progress, and went on to other things.

In the meantime Kaye and I traveled to Italy, spending time in Rome and Florence and other places of interest. In Florence we viewed Michelangelo's sculptures housed in the Galleria dell'Accademia. There you walk a long corridor that is lined with Michelangelo's "Prisoners," those unfinished figures who appear to be trying to escape from the rough marble. The feeling you get of incompleteness or unrealized potential is palpable. Then, suddenly, you come into the large open area in which the glorious David stands brilliantly exposed under a circular skylight. There you stand in awe, gazing at the most beautiful piece of sculpture ever created.

One night a few weeks later, back home in Cape Girardeau, I was working on a Faulkner essay that didn't seem to be going anywhere. So, as I typically do when a writing project stalls, I closed that computer file and searched for another to work on. Quite by chance, I opened the file on "Swoboda," read what I had written, and, almost immediately, found my ending.

The poem, I now recognized, was about the potential I had seen in an eleventh grade athlete at Sparrows Point High School who had gone on to star for the "Miracle Mets," making the game-saving catch in Game 4 of the 1969 World Series. I had previously brought the poem to the point in which the young Swoboda stands in for batting practice against the pitches of the assistant coach. But now I had the concluding description of him that I thought captured a young athlete's dreaming: "like one of Michelangelo's prisoners / yearning to be a David."

There's a footnote to this story—for me an unhappy one. When "Swoboda" was included in my collection of sports poems, *Keeping*

Score, I allowed the editor of the manuscript to persuade me that my ending of the poem was perhaps "too academic" for the general readers who were the target audience for the book. So I rewrote the conclusion, changing the last two lines to read: "bat arched in readiness / aiming toward the sky." Those lines also work to suggest potential and desire, but I shall always prefer the ending of the poem I found in Florence. And I shall always be grateful to L.D. for teaching me that the act of *writing* a poem can be just as exciting and fulfilling as *completing* one.

Another important lesson that L.D. taught me was that a book of poems should not be a random collection but rather have an overall unity of focus, subject, and theme. Each individual poem should be viewed as a "chapter" in the complete work, just as a chapter of a novel contributes to the larger subject and effect of the novel. Sheri Vandermolen, who edited the multivolume *The Complete Poems of Louis Daniel Brodsky* and authored the editorial guides for those volumes, believes that L.D.'s youthful experimentations with the novel form influenced his notion that a book of poems should have an overall unity. Each of L.D.'s poetry volumes has a central focus: the day-to-day experiences of a traveling salesman, the birth and growth of his children, impressions of Faulkner's Mississippi, reflections on the Iraq war, the horror of the Holocaust, memories of his parents, the early love poems to Jan and the later ones to Jane and Linda, the satirical portraits of "rednecks," the descriptions of summer camp on Lake Nebagamon, his year-long battle with cancer. All of L.D.'s books are mosaics of individual poems strategically arranged to develop a common theme.

I initially learned this lesson on overall unity the hard way.

The original manuscript of my first book of poems, *From the Ground Up*, treating the coming of age of a young Southerner, included a section of a half dozen sports poems. When L.D. reviewed the manuscript for me, he advised me to drop the sports poems, since they didn't fit the overall theme and content of the book. He softened the criticism by suggesting that those poems might provide the nucleus for a complete book of sports poems. Though it was hard for me to remove those poems from the manuscript, L.D. proved right on both counts. Those poems didn't belong in *From the Ground Up*, and they did become, several years later, a part of *Keeping Score*.

I wish I could claim a reciprocal influence on L.D.'s poetry, but I cannot. He credited me for the title of one of his books, *The Thorough Earth*, and I fondly recall the day we sat together over cups of coffee at a local restaurant and rearranged the poems for his *Mississippi Vistas* (he accepted my advice on which should be the concluding poem in the volume). But I'm afraid I was always the student, too seldom the teacher, in our relationship as poets. In our Faulkner work, we thought of ourselves as equal partners; with the poetry I was ever the disciple.

I did, however, try to repay my poetic debt to L.D. in other ways. *Keeping Score* is dedicated to him, as "poet, scholar, athlete, and best friend." And he occasionally appears in my poems—sometimes named, sometimes not. One such poem is the following:

That November Afternoon
      —For L.D. Brodsky and Changlei Li

Remember the afternoon
when the three of us
sat around a library table,
surrounded by five centuries
of rare books,
and talked of poetry—you,
the Chinese visiting professor
who had become our friend, and I?
"What kind of poet are you?"
Changlei asked, recording notes
for his introduction
to a Chinese translation of your poems,
and I, trying to be helpful, said,
"Call him a heartland poet—
a poet of mid-America,
and of the land of the heart."

And later that same afternoon
when we walked to the river,
jogging the last two blocks down the hill
after we heard the blast
of the riverboat's whistle
and caught a glimpse
through the floodwall gate
of the Mississippi Queen
leaving the dock?

You, lover of riverboats,
wanted to watch the boat
paddlewheel away from the landing,
savor every sound and ripple,
as it moved to the middle of the river,
reversed its course,
and headed south toward Cairo,
Memphis, Natchez, New Orleans.
Changlei was busily fussing
with his camera, frantic to capture
every detail of the scene on film,
snapping shots of the boat,
passengers waving from the deck,
spectators lining the riverfront,
you and me.

Was it our burning talk of poetry
from opposite sides of the earth,
or the poetry of the scene before us,
or the gathering of three friends
that made the day so memorable?
No matter,
we both have now written poems
to celebrate the occasion,
and somewhere today in China,
in an album of snapshots
or perhaps framed on a friend's wall,
is a photograph of us
standing beside the moving water
carrying the boat, and the moment,
away and beyond us, out of time
into the sweet, bending curve of memory.

In 2008, I presented a paper at the annual College English Association's meeting on one of my favorites among L.D.'s books, *You Can't Go Back, Exactly*, a retrospective treatment of his youthful days spent at a summer camp located on Lake Nebagamon in northern

Wisconsin. Since the CEA met that year in St. Louis, I invited L.D. to the session in which I presented. In the paper, I traced L.D.'s treatment of such themes as the beauty of nature, youthful innocence versus adult awareness, and the redemptive power of memory and art. I concluded by predicting that L.D. undoubtedly wasn't finished with the subject of Lake Nebagamon—that, given his typical practice, he would return to these poems and probably even write additional poems on the same subject. In the lively discussion that followed my presentation, L.D. contradicted me on that claim. He had had his say on Nebagamon; there would be no more poems on that topic.

I laughed off his comment. "This is a new experience for me," I told the audience. "William Faulkner has never quarreled with anything I've ever said about him."

Of course I was right and L.D. was wrong about my contention, as subsequent developments proved: he afterward published two additional volumes of Lake Nebagamon poems. Like Whitman, L.D. was seldom finished with an individual poem or a subject. There was always another possible revision to be made or a further word to be said.

One of the great delights of interacting over the years with "POET--LD" (the identification on his Corvette's license plate) was the occasional joy of receiving a poem from him celebrating some event in the life of my family or some occasion or happening he and I had shared.

In 2003, Kaye and I moved out of the small, split-level house we had lived in for thirty-eight years and into a decaying, three-story, Queen Anne Victorian house that we restored and placed on the National Register of Historic Places. L.D. loved to visit us in this house, in part I think because the house reminded him of the huge, steamboat Gothic house he and his family lived in for several years in Farmington. As a housewarming gift, he presented us with a beautiful pump organ with ornate crown—the very first antique he had purchased in his earlier avatar as antique collector. Two lovely paintings that hang on our walls are also gifts from L.D.

The guest bedroom that L.D. used on his overnight visits with us contains a large stained-glass window designed, like each of the five stained-glass windows in the house, around a scarab beetle motif. When the rising sun flows through the window, the entire room is bathed in gorgeous colors. On one of his visits, L.D. penned the following poem and presented it to us. A framed copy of it now sits on the night table beside the bed in that room.

Scarab
For Kaye and Bob Hamblin, with my love

In Egyptian mythology,
The scarab symbolizes immortality—
A mere beetle, ugly to the common eye,

Idolized, nonetheless, by pharaohs and high priests,
Who would take several along, into the other world,
In accompaniment to their divinity.

Last night, in a red-brick Victorian house,
In Cape Girardeau,
I, too, fell into a semblance of that ageless sleep,

Watched over by a stained-glass scarab,
Poised above my head,
Whose amber, green, blue, and red body

Bathed my weary spirit
When morning's annealing rays slanted through,
Awakened me to the glory of a new sun

Waiting for my soul to enter its halo
And follow that scarab
Into the promise of an eternal day.

In 2013, just months before he died, L.D. donated his entire poetry archives to Southeast Missouri State University—a fitting complement to his Faulkner collection. Filling a dozen large file cabinets, each holding hundreds of file folders, the archives contains all of his published volumes and multiple drafts of the 13,000 poems written over a fifty-year period. Like his Faulkner collection, the poetry archives will be made available to students and scholars for reading, study, and research.

The formal opening of the Louis Daniel Brodsky Poetry Archives was held on September 8, 2016. I expect to be one of its most frequent visitors.

Summing Up

As of this writing, in early 2017, I have been involved with William Faulkner, in one fashion or another, for fifty-eight years. My association and collaboration with L.D. Brodsky lasted for thirty-six years. I have been greatly blessed by my relationships with both.

These days, graduate students in literature are advised not to focus their research on a particular writer but rather to examine broader issues of literary history and culture. This is partly because in a shrinking job market, with fewer tenure-track positions being offered in specialized studies, students are better served by being prepared to teach a wider range of authors and subjects.

I agree with this approach. The last thing I wanted to be, in literature or in life, was a specialist. The world is too big a house to spend all of one's time in a single room.

I was very fortunate in my choice of graduate schools, the Ph.D. program at the University of Mississippi. Even though my principal interest was American literature, I was required to study English literature and language as well. Thus, in addition to courses in American poetry, fiction, and drama, I also took courses in Shakespeare, Chaucer, Milton, Old and Middle English, the Renaissance, the Eighteenth Century, the Romantic Age, the Victorian Age, and the History of the English Language.

When it came time for my job search, I didn't apply to a single Ph.D.-granting institution, since I was more interested in teaching than in doing research in a "publish or perish" environment. I settled on Southeast Missouri State University, where for the next fifty years I taught principally undergraduate students in a variety of classes, including American literature survey courses and the Twentieth-Century American Novel, but also such classes as Shakespeare, English Literature surveys, Literary Criticism, Utopias and Dystopias, the Bible in Literature, and the Literature of Sport—and, of course, the required courses in English Composition. I am especially grateful for my English literature classes at Ole Miss, since those courses on my transcript qualified me to teach in the Missouri London Program on two separate occasions.

My writing likewise reflects a variety of interests. I've published, in addition to my work with L.D., six volumes of poetry, three biographies (one of a basketball coach), three memoirs, several short stories, personal essays on sports, and scholarly books or articles on Shakespeare, Mark Twain, Kate Chopin, Toni Morrison, Robert Penn Warren, Pat Conroy, Isaac Singer, and W.P. Kinsella, as well as Faulkner.

It was only after L.D. Brodsky entered my life that I became a "Faulkner specialist." And even then, my reading of and writing about Faulkner have always been done in a broad humanistic context as opposed to a narrow specialization. For undergraduates, I prefer general education (at our school called "University Studies," a program which I helped to develop) to specialized study, and I believe that every major or specialty should be connected to a wider range of knowledge and experience. All of the greatest authors, I would argue (and I include Faulkner in that group), are humanists, not specialists.

And what I have most learned from Faulkner in my fifty-eight years in his company fits this humanistic mold.

It can be argued that the overarching themes of all of Faulkner's works relate to time and consequent change. The history of Faulkner's Yoknapatawpha stretches from the arrival of the white settlers on the Mississippi frontier in the early 1800s to the beginnings of the civil rights movement in the 1940s. In between are stories that relate to the antebellum plantation world supported by chattel slavery, the Civil War and emancipation, Reconstruction, Jim Crow, the decline of the old aristocracy and the rise of the yeoman farmers of the middle and lower classes, World Wars I and II, the Great Depression, and "the Bulldozer revolution" (as C. Vann Woodward called the mechanization and industrialization of the South).

Caught in this world of continual change that produces a great degree of uncertainty and ambivalence, the Faulkner character (and reader) must weigh the traditions of the past with the demands of the present and the future. Faulkner's tragic characters—such as Quentin Compson, Gail Hightower, Emily Grierson, Thomas Sutpen, Temple Drake, and Ike McCaslin—are those who cannot escape the past, cannot accept the changes required to adapt to a new world, or—like Joe Christmas and Caddy Compson—are victimized by those who cannot accept change. Other characters, the successful ones it seems to me—like Dilsey Gibson, Lena Grove, Byron Bunch, V.K. Ratliff, Sarty Snopes, Chick Mallison, Linda Snopes, and Lucius Priest—prove willing and able to navigate the sometimes turbulent waters caused by the conflict of the past and present, tradition and progress.

Bayard Sartoris of *The Unvanquished* provides an example of a Faulkner character who successfully resolves this conflict of culture versus change. The heart and climax of this novel is the final chapter, "An Odor of Verbena," which Faulkner also published as a separate short story and which is one of his finest narratives. Set in 1875, "An Odor of Verbena" dramatizes the inner conflict of Bayard, a twenty-four-year-old law student, as he contemplates his response to the murder of his father by a former business partner named Redmond. As Bayard well knows, one part of the historical tradition that has nurtured him requires that he avenge his father's death. In fact, Bayard himself had previously participated in a revenge killing—that of Grumby for the murder of Granny Millard. However, another part of Bayard's tradition, based on the biblical assertions "Thou shalt not kill" and "Who lives by the sword shall die by it," argues against revenge. Moreover, as a law student, Bayard now understands the difference between legal process and vigilante action. In determining his response to his father's death, Bayard must decide which part of his tradition he will obey.

Drusilla, Bayard's stepmother, becomes the dominant voice advocating the code of vengeance. As he rides the forty miles to Jefferson from the university, Bayard foresees Drusilla waiting for him, wearing a sprig of verbena, her symbol of courage, and offering in her outstretched hands the two dueling pistols. To Bayard she seems "the Greek amphora priestess of a succinct and formal violence." However, as the reader soon discovers, Bayard has already determined that he will refuse the weapons. He will face his father's enemy as the revenge code, and his own integrity, require, but he will go unarmed. This decision demonstrates that while Bayard has rejected the violence of the revenge code, he has retained and acted upon that part of the same code that insists upon personal courage and family honor. This paradox underscores what Faulkner perceives to be the complex relationship of every individual to an inherited tradition. Bayard does not—indeed cannot—divorce himself from that tradition; instead, he immerses himself in it, judges it, and adopts as his own those parts of the tradition that best serve his own personal code.

In his novels and stories, William Faulkner sought to explore, honestly and faithfully, the ambivalent and delicate relationship that exists between every individual and his or her society. Although Faulkner recognizes that the specific issues and questions will change from one generation or culture to the next, he believed there are certain general principles that apply to all situations. The overriding principle is that all issues must be considered in the context of a genuine concern for ethical, moral values, for what Faulkner called "the old verities and truths of the heart," specifically, "love and honor and pity and pride and compassion and sacrifice." Thus it is not enough just to be able, like Jason Compson and Flem Snopes, to adapt to a changing world; one must be careful not to forfeit one's soul in doing so. In order to be faithful to such "verities," we must never allow our allegiance to our society to blind us to its shortcomings and failings. At the same time, a hatred for those traditions and practices that are contemptible should never seduce us into betraying those elements in our personal and cultural history that are positive and good. As the content and form of Faulkner's fiction imply, only the individual can decide which aspects of any tradition are deemed worth preserving; it is left to each of us to discover, even to fashion, as best we can, our own voice out of the many voices that float through our mind and experience. As Faulkner acknowledges, this process of discovery and growth is a difficult and sometimes painful one; yet to engage in that quest is to realize the very essence of what it means to be human.

There's a song that we still occasionally hear on the radio about a gambler who reminds us that it's important to identify the difference between what is worth keeping and what should be thrown away. This notion sums up for me the aspect of Faulkner's work that is perhaps the most useful to contemporary readers. Faulkner well knew, from his deep immersion in the history and culture of the American South, that some cards are not worth holding, and the player who holds them will do so to his detriment and sorrow. But Faulkner also realized that it is hardly advisable to throw away all the cards. The secret to surviving is learning which cards to throw away and which to keep. This, I believe, is one of the lessons Faulkner tried to teach his fellow Southerners in his time. It is now one of the lessons his books teach all of us, whatever our backgrounds or traditions. It's a lesson, I am convinced, that we would ignore to our peril.

Now, in conclusion, what shall I add about L.D. Brodsky? In previous sections of this essay, I have discussed L.D.'s influence upon me as a collector/scholar and as a poet. But there still remains something to be said about L.D., the man.

When I first met L.D. in 1978, I quickly became aware that we came from two vastly different worlds. He was a city boy; I grew up in the country. His father was a wealthy St. Louis businessman; mine was, successively, a Mississippi sharecropper, country store owner, and truck driver. L.D. was a graduate of Country Day, a prestigious private school in St. Louis, and Yale University; I was a graduate of a small-town public school, a community college, and a tiny state college. I was primarily an academic; he was a businessman who was also a poet.

Yet, despite our differences, we almost immediately bonded, initially because of our mutual interest in Faulkner but ultimately because we genuinely liked each other and enjoyed being in one another's company. We were both, as it turned out, "workaholics" (he already was one; I became one), and we fed off each other's energy and enthusiasm. "Follow your bliss," Joseph Campbell, the famous mythologist, once said, "and the universe will open doors where there were only walls"; and L.D. and I seemed able to inspire one another along that pathway. Do what makes you happy; and be happy and grateful in the doing of it. In the process of that shared pursuit we became more than friends—in fact, something more like brothers.

I grew up with two sisters, and while I dearly love both of them, I always regretted not having a brother. Actually, there was another boy in our family, James Robert, but he died at only two years of age and two years before I was born. Years later, when a caseworker interviewed Kaye and me in the adoption process for our first child, I was asked, "Were you ever made to feel by your parents that you were a replacement for the child that died?" I could honestly answer that question with a no, but from time to time in my childhood and youth, James Robert would be mentioned by my parents or my sisters, and always, when I heard his name, I would try to imagine what it would be like had the brother I never knew survived.

I remember too that once, when I was bullied on the playground by an older schoolmate, I had blurted out through tears, "If my brother were still alive, you wouldn't treat me like this." I still don't know where that statement came from, but apparently, as I reflect on it now, it resonated from some profound psychological need deep within my psyche.

But I never had a brother—until William Faulkner gave me one.

Ideally, brothers stick together through thick and thin. They are loyal to one another, and they encourage and support each other's dreams and aspirations. They delight in each other's successes and console one another in their disappointments and failures. They are there for each other, in good times or bad. They laugh together and grieve together. They love one another.

L.D. Brodsky was this kind of brother for me, as I hope I was for him. What a marvelous, richly rewarding journey we traveled together.

POSTSCRIPT

L.D. died on June 16, 2014, at his home in St. Louis after a year-long battle with brain cancer. Following the initial diagnosis of a brain tumor in early 2013, he underwent surgery to have the tumor removed, but the procedure left him with diminished capacity in speech and an inability to write. Remarkably, however, once chemo and physical-therapy treatments were begun, he regained some of his power of speech, and he was able to resume writing, although the effort required was terribly difficult and extremely tiring. Assisted by his longtime editor, Jerry Call, and able to write sometimes no more than two hours per day, L.D. set to work to produce a day-by-day chronicle of his terminal illness. The resultant series of 294 poems, titled *The Words of My Mouth and The Meditations of My Heart*, is a powerful statement of the triumph of the human spirit over tragedy and despair, a profound "saying No to death" that William Faulkner said is the aim and hope of every writer. In the endorsement L.D. asked me to write after reviewing a draft of the manuscript, I wrote: "In these moving and insightful poems modeled after the Book of Psalms, Louis Daniel Brodsky, gravely ill, looks Death squarely in the face and answers with a series of unyielding affirmations—a faith in God, faith in human relationships, faith in life's precious passing moments, and, undergirding and supporting all of these, faith in the power and beauty of the poetic voice."

Following the completion of his personal Book of Psalms, which would be published just days before he died, a second brain tumor developed that proved resistant to all forms of treatment and therapy, and L.D. was placed in hospice care. During his final days he declined to see visitors, allowing only his immediate family, his beloved associates at Time Being Books, and his caregivers into his presence.

I last saw L.D. four months before he died. Kaye and I drove to St. Louis to visit with him. I had rushed during the final months of his fatal illness to complete a first draft of *My Life with Faulkner and*

Brodsky, and I presented a copy of the manuscript to him, knowing that in all likelihood he would never be well enough to read it. He accepted the manuscript, held it lovingly in his hands, and expressed gratitude that I had documented the history of our collaboration. Accompanying us on the trip were Changlei Li and his wife Xiumei, both of whom had returned to Cape Girardeau for a second tenure of study at the Faulkner Center. Changlei also had a gift for L.D.—a beautiful Chinese/English edition of a selection of L.D.'s nature poems that Changlei and his translation students had prepared.

Kaye and I attended L.D.'s funeral, a simple graveside service in B'nai Amoona Cemetery in St. Louis. Rabbi Amy Feder of Congregation Temple Israel, St. Louis, directed the service and presented the Mourner's Kaddish. L.D.'s daughter and son, Trilogy and Troika; his sisters, Barbara and Dale; and his brother, Jeffrey, delivered the eulogies. At the end of the service, L.D.'s casket was slowly lowered into the ground beside the graves of his parents, Saul and Charlotte Brodsky; and family and friends performed the symbolic final act of love and friendship by tossing a shovelful of dirt onto the coffin. As I took my turn, I offered a silent plea that L.D.'s prayer in the final stanza of the final poem in his final book would be answered:

> Each evening, when I go to bed,
> I hope and pray that my awakened soul,
> For eternities everlasting to everlasting, will read, to my dreams,
> The meditations gathered over this preceding year's pilgrimage,
> So that I'll always sleep the peaceful deep sleep
> Of the ages, sages, and patriarchs
> And ceaselessly rest the stressless rest
> Of my blessed ancestors,
> With their unwavering faith in YHWH.

Acknowledgments

There are countless people to thank for a book describing a long career of pleasurable work. Since many of them play a significant role in the narrative and thus have already been identified, I will simply add: my heartfelt thanks to each of you for your support and encouragement over the years.

But I must make special mention of the following: all of my friends and colleagues at Southeast Missouri State University but especially Bill Stacy, Les Cochran, James Zink, Fred Goodwin, Henry Sessoms, Jane Stephens, Martin Jones, Robert Burns, and Carol Scates; the successive directors of the Faulkner and Yoknapatawpha Conference at the University of Mississippi: Evans Harrington, Ann J. Abadie, Donald Kartiganer, and Jay Watson; and the longtime director of the Southeast Missouri State University Press, Susan Swartwout (who graciously worked past her retirement to copyedit this book); her successor, James Brubaker; and their assistant, Carrie Walker.

My collaboration with L.D. Brodsky would not have been possible without the understanding and patience of Kaye Hamblin and Jan Brodsky. "They endured."

My greatest indebtedness is to Louis Daniel Brodsky, for his trust, friendship, loyalty, and dedication. What a man! What a friend! *Shalom, chaver.*